DATE DUE			
Nov 15, 79			

STUDIES IN ENGLISH LITERATURE

Volume XCVI

LE MORTE ARTHUR
A Critical Edition

by

P. F. HISSIGER
Manhattan College

1975
MOUTON
THE HAGUE · PARIS

ISBN 90 279 3211 5

Printed in Belgium by N.I.C.I., Ghent.

CONTENTS

INTRODUCTION

DESCRIPTION OF MS

Le Morte Arthur survives in a unique manuscript in the British Museum, Harleian 2252, leaves 86 recto to 133 verso. The manuscript is a paper folio, measuring 7-5/8 inches by 11 inches. The section containing the romance is composed of three quires, and is on paper bearing two distinct watermarks. Most of the paper was milled at Palermo in 1465:[1] the rest is similar to paper milled in France, and to a lesser extent in Germany and the Low Countries, between 1481 and 1525.[2] The first is found on eighteen folios, the second on five. One folio is missing, between lines 1181 and 1318.

Although the manuscript seems to have been rebound into its present binding since it was acquired by the British Museum in 1753, it was very possibly bound into its present order about 1517. It was the miscellaneous collection of John Colyns, a London merchant, whose statement at the end of *Le Morte Arthur* is dated 1517. The first letters of many words in Colyns' statement, the poem itself, and many other parts of the collection are tinted in the same red ink. In addition, the first letter of line one, "L" is entirely in that ink. The tinting is neither complete nor consistent, but it must have been done at about the same time, and after the book was compiled. Many stanzas begin with two or three

---

[1] C. M. Briquet, *Les Filigranes: dictionnaire historique des marques du papier* (Geneva, 1907), No. 3537.
[2] Briquet, Nos. 1744, 1746, and 1748.

indented lines to leave room for a large initial letter, but the red "L" is the only one supplied.

The romance was written down by two scribes, the first copying up to 101V and the second from 102R to the end. The first scribe wrote in a large clear hand, using a lighter ink than the second. He also used the m/n superscript more often than the second, thirty-seven times to the second scribe's thirteen in many more lines, but the second scribe's superscripts are always clearly intended and some of the first's are open to question. The first scribe always writes out his numbers, whereas the second frequently uses numerals. In addition, the second writes in a smaller, more cramped, and more flourishing hand, and has many more corrections than the first. He is also responsible for all the non-functional marginalia. He may have been less experienced than the first, or at any rate, less successful: he writes at the end, "so more I can", as though he were looking for more work.

The marginalia are as follows:

101V. At the bottom right margin, "for trew" is written to indicate where the scribe should begin the next page. Below that is an "a" indicating the end of a quire.

116V. In the left margin, at the upper middle of the page, what appears to be "Mary" is written. It is ornate, and not in the hand of either scribe. It runs off the page and has partly blotted onto 117R. In the lower right hand corner, "Arthur" is written to show where to begin the next page and below that a "B" to indicate the end of a quire.

119V. "Ihesu mercy" is written at the top, centered over the text.

121R. "Ih" is written at the top, centered over the text.

126R. There are dots and scribbling all along the upper right margin.

126V. "ihesu mert" is written at the top, centered over the text.

133V. Centered below the text, "Explycit" is written twice, then below to the left "amen", and to the right "so more I can". All this is in the second scribe's hand. Below, in a larger hand, is written, "Thys boke belongythe to John Colyns, mercer, of London, dwelling in the parysshe of Our Lady of Wolchyrchehawe anexid the stocks in þe Pultre, yn anno domine 1517." The church stood on part of the site now occupied by Mansion House in London; it was destroyed in the Great Fire in 1666.

DIALECT AND DATE

Until Paul Seyferth's study in 1895, there was no systematic attempt to determine the date of *Le Morte Arthur*. Scholars' guesses placed it as early as the reign of Edward II[3] or as late as the reign of Henry VII.[4] Seyferth placed the poem in the fourteenth century, at the latest 1400, and pointed to words such as "fele" (6, 2019, 2032, 2157, 2223), "lede" (653, 2659, 3163), "blee" (739, 1544, 3504, 3779, 3876), and "wynne" (1830), which he held had disappeared even in northern England by the beginning of the fifteenth century.[5] With few exceptions,[6] the fourteenth century is generally accepted as the date of the poem.

Seyferth was also the first scholar to take a systematic look at the dialect of *Le Morte Arthur*. He concluded that the poet was from the northern border of the West Midlands, and the scribes were from the East Midlands, the second from the southern border of the East Midlands.[7] Despite the problems presented by the erratic spelling in the manuscript and the inexact rhymes in the poem, Seyferth seems to have been quite thorough and accurate.

[3] Thomas Warton, *History of English Poetry* (1871 ed.) as quoted in J. Douglas Bruce (ed.) *Le Morte Arthur* (EETSES 88; London, 1903), p. viii.
[4] Humphrey Wanley, *Catalogue of the Harleian Manuscripts* (London, 1808) II, 584; Joseph Ritson, *Ancient Engleish Metrical Romanceës* (London, 1802), I, cvi.
[5] Paul Seyferth, *Sprache und Metrik des Mittelenglischen Strophischen Gedichtes "Le Morte Arthur" und sein Verhältnis zu "The Lyfe of Ipomydon"* (Berliner Beitrage zur Germanischen und Romanischen Philologie, VIII; Berlin), p. 58.
[6] Charles Moorman, *The Book of King Arthur* (Lexington: University of Kentucky Press, 1965), p. xviii refers to *Le Morte Arthur* as a fifteenth century poem. As he makes no attempt to prove this date, it may have been an inadvertent error.
[7] Seyferth, pp. 58-59.

In his summary of Seyferth's points on the dialect of the poet, J. Douglas Bruce notes that "there" and "were" are spelled with both *a* and *e*, and in two instances pronounced *o*. He states this mixture is characteristic of the North and North Midlands.[8] Actually, *there* is spelled all three ways (see 409, 415; 154, 160; 316, 1342), as are *ere* (see 2013; 291, 977; 1740, 2202) and *swore* (see 432, 1604; 469, 486; 1725). While we do face the problems of inexact rhyming and inexact spelling here, it is important that northern forms occur in the rhymes, and very rarely elsewhere in the text. Bruce's suggestion about variant pronunciations looks suspect at first, but such things do occur. The same person today may have two distinct ways of saying such words as "either", "route", and "envelope", for example.

Among the other points in Bruce's summary are: three rhyming present participles in -and (2371, 2667, 2840), and only one in -yng (3676); all rhyming second person present indicative inflections but one in -s; *was* appears to be pronounced *wes* in rhymes; infinitives are not inflected, except for *sayne* (987, 1106, 1587, 1672, 3319), *slayne* (1591, 3327), *bene* (1503), and *sene* (725); the northern past participle *drayne* is used (859, 1850, 1997, 2164, 3014), and so is the ending in -(e)n in rhymes.[9] West Midland forms such as *lond* (995, 2665, 2836, 3560), *hond* (2661, 2838, 3564), and *stond* (2663, 2941) also occur, but they are rhymed with -and and -ound endings. Among the northern and Scandinavian words noted by Seyferth, Bruce takes as the strongest: *fone* (2378), *sitte* (497, 870), *to* meaning until (374, 3437), *sprente* (1846, 1892, 1949, 1954, 1994), *glente* (3493), *thro* (589, 1525, 2184, 2389, 2879), *layne* (602, 1964, 3204; 989, 1026, 1108), *busk* (349, 547, 699, 1808, 2151), *graythe* (2530, 2739), and *bayne* (991, 1134, 3217, 3315).[10] Another northern word found in the poem is *tase* for *takes* (956).

The poet's dialect area may also show in the heavy use of alliteration. Seyferth calculated that 42 percent of the lines in the

---

8   Bruce, pp. xxi-xxii.
9   Bruce, pp. xxii-xxiii.
10   Bruce, p. xxiii.

romance contain alliteration.[11] The so-called alliterative revival of the fourteenth century is, of course, generally held to have taken place in the North and North West Midlands. One of the points in William Matthews' argument for a northern Thomas Malory, moreover, is that Malory actually increased the amount of alliteration in *Le Morte Arthur* when using it as a source.[12] Indeed, Howard Maynadier suggested the poem was originally alliterative,[13] but such a complicated history is scarcely likely. If, as Matthews suggests, the habit of alliteration could be carried into prose, it could just as easily have been carried into metrical verse. All this would seem to support the argument that the poet was from the North West Midlands.

Seyferth seems to be correct, too, in identifying the dialects of the scribes. The first scribe has *o* rather than the northern *a* in *old* (3, 103), *stone* (115, 590, 761), *woe* (80, 652, 759), *none* (164, 295, 638, 767, 1076 etc.), *sore* (335, 424, 500, 543, 631 etc.), and he has *a* rather than West Midland *o* in *land* (436, 801, 920), *man* (853), and *answer* (368). *They*, *their*, and *them* are written only in their th- form, which is generally taken to be the northern or North East Midlands form. *She* is written only that way, which is characteristic of the East Midlands. Finally, he inflects all present tense, third person singular and first person plural verbs in northern -es. This combination suggests that he was from the Northern East Midlands. The main difference between the two scribes is their spelling of *them* and *their*. The second scribe uses *them* thirty times (1661, 2188, 2257, 2260, 1308 etc.) and *hem* sixty-four times (1165, 1166, 1330, 1445, 1464 etc.), *their* twenty times (1500, 1671, 1893, 1922, 1932, etc.), and *here* thirteen times (1333, 1537, 1723, 1870, 1871 etc.). This would indicate that the second scribe was from a part of the Midlands closer to the southern dialect area.

---

[11] Seyferth, p. 61.

[12] William Matthews, *The Ill-framed Knight* (Berkeley: University of California Press, 1966), pp. 97, 236-237.

[13] Howard Maynadier, *The Arthur of the English Poets* (Boston, 1907), p. 213. Matthews says, "No one has ever suggested that it is necessary to postulate a variant form of the stanzaic poem", p. 237.

METER AND FORM

Le Morte Arthur is written for the most part in eight line stanzas, with four accents to the line. The prevailing rhythm is iambic. The usual rhyme scheme in full stanzas is abababab, but the first stanza rhymes ababcbcb, two other stanzas rhyme ababbaba, and five others, abababac. Three of the stanzas have only seven lines, six have only six lines, and one, only four lines. All but one of the short stanzas were copied by the second scribe, and are probably errors by him. The stanzas are not separated in the manuscript nor in the earlier editions. Bruce's edition is the first to divide the stanzas, but such a division is clearly indicated by the rhyme scheme. As I noted earlier, there are numerous inexact rhymes, many due to the scribes. Bruce does point out, however, some which can clearly be traced to the poet: lines 712 ff., 761 ff., 808 ff., 2818 ff., 2979 ff., 3223 ff., 3288 ff., 3320 ff., and 3392 ff. He also points out the frequent occurrance of rhymes such as -f, -th, and -gh rhyming together.[14]

THE STORY

Le Morte Arthur seems to be the oldest extant version of the popular Lancelot-Guinevere-Arthur story in English. While we cannot know if the story existed in English before, the poem does assume that its audience already knows the story. It does not provide background information, assumes the relationships of the characters one to another is understood, and generally keeps its exposition to a minimum. This may indicate, to be sure, that the poet felt his audience already knew the story from French versions, or that he was simply so used to ballad style that he adapted many of its characteristics to this verse romance. There are certainly many suggestions of ballad style in *Le Morte Arthur*: the meter itself suggests it, and so do the limited number of rhyme words and the repetition of formulae, though that is not systematic as in ballads. In addition, while there is relatively little exposition,

14 Bruce, pp. xxvi-xxvii.

what we are told is often made quite clear. Arthur's voyage to Avalon, for example, is explained fully and rather practically, and its failure is also made clear. The misty fairyland quality of most versions is almost totally missing here.

Another thing this poem has in common with ballads is something found in all popular hero literature from the epic at the highest level to the modern comic book and television serial at the lowest. This is its presentation of its hero. The hero of the poem is without a doubt, Lancelot; despite its title, it is his story rather than Arthur's, or even Arthurian society's. Lancelot's arrivals are usually greeted with great joy, with people running out to meet him or dropping to their knees to offer prayers of thanksgiving; his departures are usually occasions of sorrow and consternation. Indeed, when Guinevere is seeking someone to defend her from Mador's charges, some of the knights refuse her because she caused Lancelot to leave the court, not because they thought her in the wrong. Whenever Lancelot wants people to act more naturally than they would if they knew him, he has to assume a disguise. Accordingly, on the road to Astolat, he pretends to be an old knight; at the tournament, he fights as an untested knight; he fights Mador as a strange knight. The special standing of Lancelot can be seen when the poet introduces him, undisguised, in 1469-1474. He is first described so that no one can doubt who he is, and then, proudly, his name is given:

> The nobleste knyght than saue thay ryde
> That ever was in erthe shape.
> Hys loreme lemyd all with pride,
> Stede and armure all was blake;
> Hys name is noght to hele and hyde,
> He hyght Syr Launcelot du Lake.

No other character in the poem is given this attention, not even the king.

When Arthur dies, as I said before, the fairy qualities of the French are cut to a minimum; when most other characters die, their passing is briefly if regretfully noted: but when Lancelot dies, his death is accompanied by visions of angels, and followed by an excessively long wake. Moreover, Arthur and his society are brought to ground some five hundred lines before the end of the poem. There can be no doubt Lancelot is the central focus of the poem.

The morality of Lancelot is based on a courtly code: He is always courteous in a fight, and bitterly regrets having to fight his lord, King Arthur. Despite Guinevere's rejection of their affair in their last meeting as sinful and the cause of Arthur's downfall, Arthur himself blames Agravain for bringing about the break with Lancelot which leads to the fall. On the whole, we are led to feel Lancelot was not wrong in loving Guinevere. After he has rescued her from the fire, he offers to fight to prove her innocent of adultery and treason. Though Arthur's answer shows some cynicism about the value of the test, I do not think the poet is necessarily cynical. Lancelot and Guinevere did not sin against the courtly code. Finally, Lancelot, whose vocation is rather questionable, dies fully in the odor of sanctity, more fully assured of entrance to heaven than anyone else. While there is the moral confusion so often found in medieval courtly works, there is no doubt that Lancelot is considered a fully deserving hero and a paragon of knightly virtue in this poem.

Of the many other versions of the story of Lancelot and Guinevere and the downfall of Arthur, three must be mentioned in connection with *Le Morte Arthur*. These are its source, the *Mort Artu*; a suggested analogue, *Li Chantari di Lancelotto*; and the work for which it was one of the sources, Malory's *Morte Darthur*. It is the connection with Malory that has been the basis of most studies of this poem.

The *Mort Artu*, one of the great cycle of prose romances in French called the Vulgate cycle, is surely the source of this romance. The freedom with which the poet handled his source, however, led many to believe that there was some lost version. As Eugene Vinaver pointed out, though, there is not enough difference between extant versions of the *Mort Artu* to indicate one so widely variant.[15] There is no need, moreover, to pretend that second rate medieval authors all slavishly followed sources and to invent lost

[15]   Eugene Vinaver, *Works of Sir Thomas Malory* (Oxford, 1947), pp. 1601-02.

sources for every free rendition of an old story. The source of *Le Morte Arthur*, then, was a version of the *Mort Artu* containing the meeting of the Queen-nun and Lancelot, as in MS Palatinus Latinus 1967.[16]

Since the English poem is shorter than the French romance, many of the changes are, of course, deletions. Right at the beginning, for example, the account of the Grail quest is omitted. Much material relating to Arthur is also dropped: many of his speeches, Fortune's speech to him on the eve of the final battle, his suspicion of Guinevere before the final break, his filling of vacancies in the Round Table, his repelling a Roman invasion, and his bringing of Gawain's body to Camelot. Gawain's role, too, is less: the explanation of his increase in strength is dropped, though the fact of the increase is kept. His early ignorance of the affair between Lancelot and Guinevere, and his attempt to keep Lancelot from falling into Agravain's trap are also omitted. Even Lancelot has some things cut: in the French, he continues the fight at Winchester after he is wounded and leads his group to victory, he is wounded by an arrow after recovering from the wound in the tournament, he meets a knight by a fountain who tells him of Mador's charge against Guinevere, he leaves his shield at the church at Camelot as a reminder of his services to Arthur, and he offers to go into voluntary exile in reparation for having killed Gaheriet. Among the other omissions from the French are Guinevere's misgivings about Mordred as steward, the detailed account of Mordred's assault on the Tower, and the seizure of power by Mordred's sons and their defeat by Lancelot.

Most of the changes and additions involve Lancelot, either directly or tangentially. In *Le Morte Arthur*, Lancelot speaks to the Maid of Astolat and her brother of her love, he is prevented by the reopening of his wounds from going to the second tournament, he is found by chance in the castle where he is recuperating, he is rebuked by Guinevere when he finally returns to Camelot

---

[16] F. Whitehead, "Lancelot's Penance", *Essays on Malory*, ed. J. A. W. Bennett (Oxford, 1963), pp. 108-109. The Palatinus Latinus 1967 interpolation can be found in *La Mort le Roi Artu*, ed. Jean Frappier (3 ed.; Paris: M. J. Minard, 1964), pp. 264-266.

and rides off, he kills all of Agravain's men but Mordred, instead
of just one as in the French. Lancelot twice defeats Gawain at
the height of his powers, rather than once, and he laments his
promise to be buried at Joyus Gard. Guinevere, too, is involved
in some changes: in the English, she urges Arthur to call a tournament, she nearly goes mad when she hears of the Maid, she is
overcome with emotion on being saved from Mador's charges,
and upbraids Gawain when he tells her he was wrong about
Lancelot and the Maid. There are numerous lesser changes, such
as the switching of Bors and Ector first in the wounding of Lancelot,
and again in the search for him after the battle of Salisbury.
In a few places too, incidents are moved: Gawain's visit to Astolat
from right after the first tournament to after Lancelot's kinsmen
have found him and the story of Mordred's treason from after
Arthur's arrival in France, to after Arthur gets word of it.

Most of these changes, I feel, show an attempt by the poet
to increase the stature of Lancelot, and to concentrate on the story
of Lancelot and Guinevere.

Li Chantari de Lancelotto was suggested as an analogue by
Jessie Weston, who thought it and *Le Morte Arthur* might both
be from the same "lost source".[17] E. T. Griffiths considers her suggestion in the introduction to his edition of the Italian work.[18]
He finds fourteen points of agreement between the English and
Italian romances, eleven of which are omissions. The other three,
that the Maid confesses her love for Lancelot on their first interview,
that Gawain goes to Astolat only once and goes alone, and that
there is a religious motive for Guinevere entering the convent do
not appear particularly significant. In addition, he finds forty
things in the Italian that are in neither the English nor the French,
and three points on which the French and the Italian agree against
the English. *Li Chantari* then is no more an analogue of *Le Morte
Arthur* than any free rendition of the *Mort Artu* must be.

The most important studies of the connection between this
poem and Malory are by Robert H. Wilson, Eugene Vinaver,

---

[17]   Jessie L. Weston, *The Chief Middle English Poets* (Cambridge, Mass.,
1914), p. 388.
[18]   E. T. Griffiths, *Li Chantari di Lancelotto* (Oxford, 1924), pp. 51, 55-73.

Talbot Donaldson, and William Matthews.[19] Scholars have long recognized that *Le Morte Arthur* and the *Mort Artu* were used by Malory as sources, but these studies show that the English poem was probably the prime source of Malory's seventh and eighth tales. Wilson, Vinaver, and Donaldson all point to many cases where Malory and *Le Morte Arthur* agree against the French, and together with Matthews, they show numerous instances of verbal agreement, where Malory quotes the stanzaic poem, or makes only slight changes. Vinaver had rejected the influence of *Le Morte Arthur* on Malory's seventh tale, rejecting eight points of agreement, but R. M. Lumiansky and Donaldson both argue that it was a source for the seventh tale, the latter showing that otherwise we must fall back on the lost source theory Vinaver had rejected elsewhere.[20]

EDITIONS

The first printing of any sizeable excerpts of *Le Morte Arthur* was in George Ellis' *Specimens* in which he printed a summary and several passages.[21] Fourteen years later, in 1819, the Roxburgh Club issued an edition printed at the expense of Thomas Ponton, for which a list of corrections appeared in the *Transactions of the Philological Society* for 1860-1861.[22] In 1864, Frederick J. Furnivall published his edition, which was the standard until J. Douglas Bruce's edition was published by EETS in 1903. There were two more printings in 1912, one for the Everyman series, and

---

[19] Robert H. Wilson, "Malory, The Stanzaic *Morte Arthur*, and the *Mort Artu*", *MP*, XXXVII (1939), pp. 129-136; Vinaver, pp. 1600-02, 1610, 1613-46; E. Talbot Donaldson, "Malory and the Stanzaic *Le Morte Arthur*", *SP*, XLVII (1950), pp. 462-470; Matthews, pp. 97, 236-237.

[20] Vinaver, pp. 1572, 1584-1589; Donaldson, pp. 460-462, 471-472; R. M. Lumiansky, "'The Tale of Lancelot and Guenevere': Suspense", in *Malory's Originality*, ed. R. M. Lumiansky (Baltimore: The Johns Hopkins Press, 1964), pp. 216-217.

[21] George Ellis, *Specimens of Early English Metrical Romances*, ed. J. O. Halliwell (London, 1848), pp. 154-187.

[22] Bruce, p. ix.

one edited by Samuel B. Hemingway. These relied entirely on Bruce, however, and were not new readings of the manuscript.

EDITORIAL POLICY

My basic aim has been to present a good, accurate, and attractive text of *Le Morte Arthur*, suitable for those who want to read it as a work of medieval literature, or to study it as a source of Malory's *Morte Darthur*. To this end, I have modernized the word divisions, the captalization, and some of the letter forms. These forms are: initial "ff" and "ss", which I have made "F" and "S", or "f" and "s", whichever was appropriate. I have also followed modern practice with "u" and "v" and "i" and "j"; the distinctions did not exist in the fifteenth century, of course, and I see no point in following the sometimes confusing whims of the scribes in this. I have expanded the various abbreviations used by the scribes, including ampersands, the n/m superscription, Jhu for Jhesu, Þ for par-, pri-, and pro-, abbreviations for þat, with, sir, and the -tis endings of certain words. I have also replaced all numerals in the text with the appropriate words.

Finally, I have kept the established line numbering despite the fact that it is faulty, to avoid confusion in citations from earlier editions. F. J. Furnivall had allotted 137 lines to the lost folio; Bruce correctly estimated the number of missing lines as between 84 and 92, but kept Furnivall's numbering in his edition.[23]

[23]   Bruce, p. x.

LE MORTE ARTHUR

Lordingis that ar leff and dere,
Lystenyth, and I shall you tell
By olde dayes what aunturis were
Amonge oure eldris þat byfelle.
In Arthur dayes, that noble kinge,   5
Byfelle aunturs ferly fele,
And I shall telle of there endinge,
That mykell wiste of wo and wele.

The knightis of the Table Round,
The Sangrayle whan they had sought,   10
Aunturs that they byfore them found
Fynisshid and to ende brought,
Their enemyes they bette and bound,
For gold onlyff they lefte them noght.
Foure yere they lyved sound   15
Whan they had these werkis wroght,

Tille on a tyme þat it byfelle
The kinge in bed lay by the quene.
Off aunturs they byganne to telle,
Many that in þat land had bene.   20
"Sir, yif that it were youre wille,
Of a wondir thinge I wold you mene,
How your courte bygynnyth to spill
Off duoghty knightis all bydene.

Syr, your honour bygynnys to falle   25
That wount was wide in world to sprede,
Off Launcelott and of other all
That evyr so doughty were in dede."
"Dame, thereto thy counsell I calle,
What were best for suche a nede?"   30

86V

"Yiff ye your honoure hold shalle,
A turnement were best to bede,

Forwhy that auntre shall bygynne
And byspoke of on every syde,
That knightis shall there worship wynne   35
To dede of armys for to ryde.
Sir, lettis thus youre courte no blynne,
But lyve in honour and in pride."
"Certys, dame," the kinge said thenne,
"Thys ne shall no lenger abyde."   40

A turnement the kinge lett bede,
At Wynchester shuld it be.
Yonge Galehod was good in nede,
The chefteyne of the crye was he,
With knightis þat were stiff on stede,   45
That ladyes and maydens might se
Who that beste were of dede
Thrughe doughtynesse to have the gre.

Knightis arme them bydene
To the turnemente to ride   50
With sheldis brode and helmys shene
To wynne grete honoure and pride.
Launcelot lefte withe the quene,
And seke he lay that ylke tyde;
For love þat was theym bytwene,   55
He made inchessoun for to abyde.

The kynge satte uppon his stede

And forthe is went uppon his way.
Sir Agraveyne for suche a nede
At home bylefte, for soth to say,   60
For men told in many a thede
That Launcelot by the quene lay.
For to take them with the dede,
He awaytes both nyght and day.

Launcelott forth wendys he   65
Unto the chambyr to the quene
And sette hym downe upon his kne,
And salues there that lady shene.
"Launcelott, what dostow here with me?
The kinge is went and þe courte bydene;   70
I drede we shall discoverid be
Off the love is us bytwene.

Sir Agravayne at home is he,
Nyght and day he waytes us two."
"Nay," he sayd, "my lady fre,   75
I ne thinke not it shall be so.
I come to take my leve of the,
Oute of courte or that I go."
"Ya swithe þat thou armyd be,
For thy dwellynge me is full woo."   80

Launcelott to his chambyr yede,
There riche atyre lay hym byfore,
Armyd hym in noble wede
Off that armure gentylly was shore,
Swerd and sheld were good at nede   85
In many batayles þat he had bore,
And horsyd hym on a grey stede
Kyng Arthur had hym yeve byfore.

Haldys he none highe way,
The knight þat was hardy and fre,   90

87R

Bot hastis bothe night and day
Faste toward that riche cite,
Wynchester it hight, for sothe to say,
There the turnament shuld be.
Kinge Arthur in a castell lay,   95
Full myche there was of gam and gle.

87V   Forwhy men wold Launcelott byhold,
And he ne wold not hymself shewe,
Wyth his shuldres gonne he fold
And downe he hangid his hede full low,   100
As he ne might his lymmys weld.
Kepit he no bugle blowe,
Wele he semyd as he were old,
Forthy ne couth hym no man knowe.

The kinge stode on a toure on highte.   105
Sir Evwayne clepis he þat tyde,
"Syr Evwayne, knowistow any wight
This knight þat rides here bysyde?"
Sir Evwayne spekis wordis right,
That ay is hend is not to hyde,   110
"Sir, it is som old knighte
Is come to se þe yonge knightis ride."

They byheld hym bothe anone
A stounde for the stedis sake.
His hors stomelyd at a stone,   115
That alle his body therewith gan shake.
The knight þan braundisshid yche a bone
As he the bridelle up gan take;
Thereby wiste they bothe anone
That it was Launcelott du Lake.   120

Kynge Arthur than spekis he
To Sir Evwayne there wordis right,
"Welle may Launcelot holden be

Off alle þe world the beste knight
Off biaute and of bounte,   125
And sithe is none so moche of myght
At every dede beste is he.
And sithe he nold it wist no wight,

Sir Evwayn, will we done hym byde;
He wenys þat we know hym noght."   130
"Sir, it is better lette hym ride,
And lette hym do as he hath thoght.
He wolle be here nere bysyde,
Sithe he þus ferre hedyr hath sought.
We shalle hym know by his dede   135
And by the hors þat he hath brought."

An erle wonnyd there besyde,
The Lord of Ascolot was hight.
Launcelot gonne thedyr ride,
And sayd he wolle there dwell all night.   140
They resseyvid hym with grete pryde;
A riche soper there was dight.
His name ganne he hele and hyde,
And sayd he was a strange knight.

Thanne had the erle sonnys two   145
That were knightis makid newe.
In þat tyme was the maner so
Whan yonge knightis shuld sheldis show,
Tille þe friste yere were agoo
To bere armys of one hewe,   150
Rede or white, yelew or bloo;
Thereby men yonge knightis knew.

As they satte at there sopere,
Launcelot to the erle spake thare,
"Sir, ys here any bachelere   155
That to the turnament wolle fare?"

88R

"I have two sonnys that me is dere,
And now that oonne is seke full sare,
So in companye þat he were,
Myne other sonne I wold were thare."   160

"Sir, and thy sonne wille thedir right,
The lenger I wolle hym abyde
And helpe hym there with all my myght
That hym none harme shall betyde."
"Sir, the semys a noble knight,   165
Courteyse and hend, is not to hyde.
At morow shall ye dyne and dight,
Togedir I rede welle þat ye ride."

"Syr, of one thinge I wolle you mynne,
And beseche you for to spede,   170
Yif here were any armure inne
That I might borow it to this dede."
"Sir, my sonne lieth seke herein;
Take his armure and his stede.
For my sonnys men shall you kenne,   175
Off rede shall be your bothis wede."

Th'erle had a doughter þat was hym dere,
Mykell Launcelott she beheld.
Hyr rode was rede as blossom on brere,
Or floure þat springith in the feld.   180
Glad she was to sitte hym nere,
The noble knight undir sheld;
Wepinge was hyr moste chere
So mykell on hym hyr herte gan held.

Up than rose þat mayden stille   185
And to hyr chamber wente she tho,
Downe uppon hir bedde she felle,
That nighe hyr herte brast in two.
Launcelot wiste what was hyr wyll,

88V

Welle he knew by other mo.   190
Hyr brother klepitte he hym tylle,
And to hyr chamber gonne they go.

He satte hym downe for the maydens sake
Upon hyr bedde there she lay.
Courtessely to hyr he spake   195
For to comforte þat fayre may.
In hyr armys she gan hym take,
And these wordis ganne she say,
"Sir, bot yif that ye it make,
Saff my lyff no leche may."   200

"Lady," he sayd, "thou moste lette,
For me ne giff the nothynge ille.
In another stede myne hert is sette;
It is not at myne owne wille.
In erthe is nothinge that shall me lette   205
To be thy knight, lowde and stille.
Another tyme we may be mette
Whan thou may better speke thy fille."

"Sithe I of the ne may have more,
As thou arte hardy knight and fre,   210
In the turnement þat thou wold bere
Sum signe of myne þat men might se."
"Lady, thy sleve thou shalte of shere,
I wolle it take for the love of the;
So did I nevyr no ladyes ere,   215
Bot one that most hathe lovid me."

On the morow whan it was day,
They dyned and made them yare,
And þan they went forthe on there way
Togedyr, as they bretherne were.   220
They mette a squyer by the way
That frome the turnament gan fare,

And askyd yif he couthe them say
Whiche party was the bygger thare.

"Sir Galehod hathe folke þe more   225
For sothe, lordingis, as I you telle,
But Arthur is the bigger there.
He hath knightis stiff and felle;
They ar bold and breme as bare,
Evwayne and Boert and Lyonelle."   230
Th'erlys sonne to hym spake thare,
"Sir, with them I rede we dwelle."

Launcelotte spake as I you rede,
"Sithe they ar men of grete valour,
How might we amonge them spede   235
There alle are stiffe and stronge in stowre?
Helpe we them þat hath most nede,
Ageyne the beste we shall welle dore;
And we might there do any dede,
It wold us torne to more honour."   240

Launcelot spekis in that tyde
As knight þat was hardy and fre,
"Tonight withoute I rede we byde,
The presse is grete in the cite."
"Sir, I have an aunte here beside,   245
A lady of swith grete biaute;
Were it your wille thedir to ride,
Glad of us than wold she be."

Tho to the castelle gonne they fare,
To the lady fayre and bright.   250
Blithe was the lady thare
That they wold dwelle with hyr þat night.
Hastely was there soper yare,
Off mete and drinke rychely dight.
Onne the morow gonne they dyne and fare,   255
Both Launcelott and þat other knight.

89V

Whan they come into þe feld,
Myche there was of game and play;
A while they hovid and byheld

90R   How Arthurs knightis rode that day.   260
Galehodis party bygan to held
On fote his knightis ar lad away.
Launcelott stiff was undyr sheld,
Thinkis to helpe yif that he may.

Besyde hym come þan Sir Evwayne,   265
Breme as any wilde bore;
Launcelott springis hym ageyne,
In rede armys þat he bare.
A dynte he yaff with mekill mayne;
Sir Evwayne was unhorsid thare,   270
That alle men wente he had bene slayne,
So was he woundyd wondyr sare.

Sir Boerte thoughte nothinge good
Whan Sir Evwayne unhorsid was;
Forthe he springis as he were wode   275
To Launcelot withouten lees.
Launcelot hytte hym on the hode;
The nexte way to ground he chese.
Was none so stiff agayne hym stode,
Fulle thynne he made the thikkest prees.   280

Sir Lyonelle beganne to tene,
And hastely he made hym bowne.
To Launcelott with herte kene,
He rode with helme and swerde browne;
Launcelott hitte hym, as I wene,   285
Throughe the helme into þe crowne,
That evyr after it was sene;
Bothe hors and man there yede adowne.

The knightis gadrid togedir thare,

And gan with crafte there counselle take: 290
Suche a knight was nevyr are,
90V   But it were Launcelot du Lake.
Bot for the sleve on his creste was thar,
For Launcelot wold they hym noght take,
For he bare nevir none suche byfore,   295
But it were for the quenys sake.

"Off Ascolot he nevyr was,
That thus welle beris hym today."
Ector sayd withouten lees;
What he was he wold assay.   300
A noble stede Ector hym chese
And forthe rydis glad and gay.
Launcelot he mette amydde þe prese;
Bytwene them was no childis play.

Ector smote with herte good   305
To Launcelot that ilke tyde,
Throughe helme into his hede it yode,
That nighe loste he all his pride.
Launcelot hytte on the hood
That his hors felle and he besyde.   310
Launcelot blyndis in his blode,
Oute of the feld full faste gan ride.

Oute of the feld they reden thoo
To a forest highe and hore,
Whan they come by them one two,   315
Off his helme he takis thore.
"Sir," he sayd, "me is full woo.
I drede that ye be hurte full sore."
"Nay," he sayd, "it is not so,
But fayne at rest I wold we were."   320

"Sir, myne aunte is here besyde
There we bothe were all nighte.

Were it youre wille thedir to ride,
She wolle us helpe with all hyr might,
And send for lechis this ylke tyde 325
Youre woundis for to hele and dight,
And I myself wille with you abyde
And be youre servante and youre knight."

To the castelle they toke the way,
To the lady fayre and hend. 330
She sent for lechis, as I you say,
That wonnyd bothe ferre and hend,
But by the morow that it was day,
In bed he might hymself not wend,
So sore woundyd there he lay 335
That well nighe had he sought his end.

Tho Kinge Arthur with mykell pride
Callid his knightis all hym by,
And sayd a mounth he wold there byde,
And in Wynchester lye. 340
Heraudis he dyd go and ride,
Another turnamente for to crye.
"This knight wolle be here nere besyde,
For he is woundyd bitterlye."

Whan the lettres made were, 345
The heraudis forth with them yede
Throughe Yngland for to fare,
Another turnament for to bede:
Bad them buske and make them yare,
Alle that stiff were on stede. 350
Thus these lettris sent were
To tho that doughty were of dede.

Tille on a tyme þat it befelle,
An heraude comys by the way,
And at the castelle a night gan dwelle 355

There as Launcelot woundyd lay,
And of the turnamente gon telle
That shuld come on the Sonday.
Launcelot sighes wondyr stille,
And sayd, "Allas and well-away,   360

91V   Whan knightis wynne worship and pride,
Som auntre shall hold me away
As a coward for to abyde.
This turnamente, for sothe to say,
For me is made this ylke tyde.   365
Thoughe I shuld dye this ylke day,
Certis I shalle thedyr ride."

The leche aunswerd also sone,
And sayd, "Syr, what have ye thought?
Alle the crafte that I have done,   370
I wene it wille you helpe right noght.
There is no man undir the mone,
By Hym þat all this world hath wroght,
Might save youre lyff to that tyme come
That ye upon your stede were brought."   375

"Certis, though I dye this day,
In my bedde I wolle not lye;
Yit had I levir do what I may
Than here to dye thus cowardelye."
The leche anone than went his way,   380
And wold no lenger dwelle hym by.
His woundis scryved, and stille he lay,
And in his bedde he swownyd thrye.

The lady wept as she were wode
Whan she sawe he dede wold be.   385
Th'erlis sonne with sory mode
The leche agayne clepis he,
And sayd, "Thou shalt have yiftis good

Forwhy þat thou wilte dwelle with me."
Craftely than staunchid he his blode,   390
And of good comforte bad hym be.

The heraude than wente on his way
At morow, whan the day was light,
Also swithe as evyr he may,
To Wynchester that ylke night.   395
He salued the kinge, for soth to say,
92R   By hym satte Syr Evwayne the knight,
And sithe he told upon his playe
What he had herd and sene with sight:

"Off alle þat I have sene with sight,   400
Wondir thought me nevir more
Thanne me dyd of a folyd knight
That in his bed lay woundid sore.
He myght not heve his hede upright
For alle the world have wonne thare;   405
For angwisshe þat he ne ride myght,
Alle his woundis scryved were."

Sir Evwayne than spekis wordis fre,
And to the kynge sayd he there,
"Certis, no cowarde knight is he.   410
Allas that he nere hole and fere.
Welle I wote þat it is he
That we alle of unhorsyd were.
The turnament is beste lette be;
For sothe that knight may not come there."   415

There turnement was than no more,
But this departith alle the prese:
Knightis toke there leve to fare,
Ichone his owne way hym chese.
To Kamelot the kynge went there,   420
There as Quene Gaynore was.

He wente have found Launcelot thare;
Away he was withouten lese.

　　Launcelot sore woundyd lay;
　　　Knightis sought hym full wyde.　　　　425
Th'erle sonne, night and day,
Was alle-way hym besyde;
Th'erle hymself whan he ryde may,
Brought hym home with mykell pride,
And made hym bothe game and play,　　　430
Tille he might bothe go and ryde.

92V　　Boerte and Lyonelle than sware,
And at the kinge there leve toke there,
Ageyne they wold come nevir mare
Tille they wiste where Launcelot were.　　435
Ector went with them thare
To seche his brodyr þat hym was dere.
Many a land they ganne through fare,
And sought hym bothe ferre and nere.

Tille on a tyme þat it byfelle　　　　　440
That they come by that ylke way,
And at the castelle at mete gan dwell
There as Launcelott woundyd lay.
Launcelot they saw, as I you telle,
Walke on the wallis hym to play.　　　　445
On knees for joye all they felle,
So blithe men they were that day.

Whan Launcelott saw tho ylke thre
That he in worlde lovyd beste,
A merier metinge might no man se,　　　450
And sithe he ledde them to reste.
Th'erle hymself glad was he
That he had gotten siche a geste,
So was the mayden feyre and fre
That alle hyr love on hym had keste.　　　455

Whan they were to soper dight,
Bordis were sette and clothis spradde,
Th'erlis doughter and the knight
Togedir was sette as he them badde.
Th'erlys sonnys, þat bothe were wight,   460
To serve them were nevir sadde,
And th'erle hymselfe with alle his myght
To make them bothe blyth and glad.

Bot Boert evyr in mynd he thoghte
That Launcelot had bene woundyd sore,   465
"Sir, were it your wille to hele it noght,
Bot telle where ye thus hurte were."
"By Hym þat alle this world hath wrought,"
Launcelot hymself swore,
"The dynte shalle be full dere bought   470
Yif evyr we may mete us more."

Ector ne liked that no wight,
The wordis that he herd there,
For sorow he loste both strength and might,
The colours changid in his leyre.   475
Boerte than sayd these wordis right,
"Ector, thou may make yvelle chere,
For sothe it is no coward knight
That thou arte of imanased here."

"Ector," he sayd, "where thou it were   480
That woundid me thus wondir sore?"
Ector aunswerd with symple chere,
"Lord, I ne wiste þat ye it wore.
A dynte of you I had there,
Felyd I nevir none so sore."   485
Sir Lyonelle by God þan swore
That "myne wolle sene be evyrmore."

Sir Boerte than answerd as tyte

93R

As knight þat wise was undir wede,
"I hope þat none of us was quite;   490
I had oon þat to ground I yede.
Sir, your brodyr shall ye not wite.
Now knowes either others dede;
Now know ye how Ector can smyte
To helpe you whan ye have nede."   495

Launcelot loughe with herte free
That Ector made so mekill sitte,
"Brother, no thinge drede thou the,
For I shalle be bothe hole and quite.
Though thou have sore woundid me,   500
Thereof I shall the nevir wite,
93V   Bot evyr the better love I the
Suche a dynte that thou can smyte."

Than uppon the thrid day
They toke there leve for to fare;   505
To the courte they wille away,
For he wille dwelle a while thare.
"Grete welle my lord I you pray,
And telle my lady how I fare,
And say I wylle come whan I may   510
And byddith hyr longe nothinge sare."

They toke there leve withouten lees
And wightely wente uppon there way;
To the courte the way they chese,
There as the Quene Genure lay.   515
The kinge to the foreste is
With knightis hym for to play;
Good space they had withouten prese,
There erand to the quene to say.

They knelyd downe byfore the quene,   520
The knightis þat were wise of lore,

And sayd they had Launcelot sene,
And thre dayes with hym were,
And how þat he had woundyd bene,
And seke he had lye full sore,   525
"Or ought longe ye shall hym sene;
He bad you longe nothynge sore."

The quene loughe with herte fre
Whan she wiste he was onlyff,
"O, worthy God, what wele is me;   530
Why ne wiste my lord it also swithe?"
To the foreste rode these knightis thre,
To the kinge it to kithe;
Jhesu Criste þan thankis he,
For was he nevir of word so blithe.   535

He klepyd Sir Gawayne hym nere,
And sayd, "Certis, that was he
That the rede armys bere;
Bot now he lyffis, welle is me."
Gawayne answerd with myld chere,   540
As he that ay was hend and fre,
"Was nevyr tithandis me so dere,
Bot sore me longis Launcelot to se."

At the kinge and at the quene
Sir Gawayne toke his leve that tyde,   545
And sithe at alle the courte bydene,
And buskis hym with mekyll pryde
Tille Ascalot withouten wene
Also faste as he might ryde.
Tille that he have Launcelot sene,   550
Night ne day ne wolle he byde.

By that was Launcelot hole and fere,
Buskis hym and makis all yare;
His leve hathe he take there.

94R

The mayden wepte for sorow and care,   555
"Sir, yif that youre willis were,
Sithe I of the ne may have mare,
Som thinge ye wolde beleve me here
To loke on whan me longith sare."

Launcelot spake with herte fre   560
For to comforte that lady hende,
"Myne armure shall I leve with the,
And in thy brothers wille I wend.
Loke thou ne longe not after me,
For here I may no lenger lend;   565
Longe tyme ne shalle it noght be
That I ne shalle eyther come or send."

Launcelot is redy for to ride,
And on his way he went forth right.
Sir Gaweyn come aftir on a tyde,   570
94V   And askis after suche a knighte.
They reseyved hym with grete pride,
A riche soper there was dight,
And sayd in herte is noght to hyde,
Away he was for fourtenyght.   575

Sir Gaweyne gon that mayden take,
And satte hym by that swete wight
And spake of Launcelot de Lake,
In alle the world nas suche a knight.
The mayden there of Launcelot spake,   580
Said all hyr love was on hym light,
"For his leman he hathe me take,
His armure I you shewe mighte."

"Now, damysselle," he sayd anone,
"And I am glad þat it is so.   585
Suche a lemman as thou haste oon,
In all this world ne be no mo.

There is no lady of flesshe ne bone
In this world so thryve or thro,
Thoughe hyr herte were stele or stone,   590
That might hyr love hald hym fro."

"But, damysselle, I beseche the,
His sheld that ye wold me shewe;
Launcelottis yif that it be,
Be the coloures I it knew."   595
The mayden was bothe hend and fre,
And ledde hym to a chambyr newe.
Launcelottis sheld she lette hym se
And all his armure forth she drewe.

Hendely than Syr Gawayne   600
To the mayden there he spake,
"Lady," he sayd withouten layne,
"This is Launcelottis sheld de Lake."
"Damesselle," he sayd, "I am full fayne
That he the wold to lemman take,   605
And I with alle my myght and mayne
Wille be thy knight for his sake."

Gawayne thus spake with that swete wight
What his wille was for to say.
Tille he was to bed idighte,   610
Aboute hym was gamme and play.
He toke his leve at erle and knight
On the morow whan it was day,
And sithen at the mayden brighte,
And forthe he wente uppon his way.   615

He nyste where þat he mighte,
Ne where that Launcelot wold lend,
For whan he was oute of sight
He was fulle yvelle for to fynd.
He takis hym the way right   620

And to the courte gon he wend.
Glad of hym was kyng and knight,
For he was bothe corteyse and hend.

Than it byfelle uppon a tyde,
The kinge stode by the quene and spake;   625
Sir Gaweyne standis hym besyde.
Ichone tille other there mone gan make
How longe they might with bale abyde
The comynge of Launcelot du Lake.
In the courte was litelle pryde,   630
So sore they sighyd for his sake.

"Certis, yif Launcelot were onlyff,
So longe fro courte he nold not be."
Sir Gawayne answerd also swithe,
"Thereof no wondir thinkith me;   635
The feyrest lady that is onlyff
Tille his lemman chosen hath he.
Is noon of us but wold be blithe,
Suche a semely for to see."

95V   The Kinge Arthur was full blythe   640
Off that tithingis for to lere,
And askid Syr Gawayne also swythe
What mayden that it were.
"Th'erlis doughter," he sayd as swithe,
"Off Ascolot, as ye may here,   645
There I was made glad and blithe;
His sheld the mayde shewid me there."

The quene than said wordis no mo,
Bot to hyr chambir sone she yede,
And downe uppon hyr bed felle so   650
That nighe of witte she wold wede.
"Allas," she sayd, "and well-a-wo,
That evyr I aught lyff in lede;

The beste body is loste me fro
That evyr in stoure bystrode stede."   655

Ladyes that aboute hyr stode
That wiste of hyr previte
Bad hyr be of comforte gode,
"Lette no man suche semblant se."
A bed they made with sory mode,   660
Therein they brought that lady fre.
Evyr she wepte as she were wode;
Off hyr they had full grete pite.

So sore seke the quene lay
Off sorow might she nevir lette.   665
Tille it felle uppon a day
Sir Lyonelle and Ector yede
Into the foreste them to play,
That floured was and braunchid swete;
And as they went by the way,   670
With Launcelot gonne they mete.

What woundyr was though they were blith
Whan they there master saw with sight,
On knees they felle also swithe,
And all they thankid God allmyght.   675
Joye it was to se and lythe
The metynge of the noble knighte;
And sithe he freyned also swithe,
"How fares my lady brighte?"

Than answerd the knightis fre,   680
And said that she was seke full sare,
"Grete doelle it is to here and se,
So mekylle she is in sorow and care;
The kinge a sory man ys he,
In courte for that ye come no mare.   685
Dede he wenys that ye be
And alle the courte both lasse and mare.

96R

Sir, were it your wille with us to fare
For to speke with the quene,
Blithe I wote wele that she ware,   690
Yif that she had you onys sene.
The kynge is mekille in sorow and care
And so ys all the courte bydene;
Dede they wene welle that ye are
Frome courte for ye so longe have bene."   695

He grauntis them at that ylke sythe
Home that he wille with them ride.
Therefore, the knightis were fulle blithe,
And busked them with mykelle pride
To the courte also swithe,   700
Nyght ne day they nold abyde.
The kinge and alle the courte was blithe,
The tydandis whan they herde þat tyde.

The kinge stode in a toure on highe,
Besydes hym standis Syr Gawayne,   705
Launcelotte whan that they sighe
Were nevir men on mold so fayne.
They ranne as swithe as evyr they might
Oute at the gates hym agayne.
Was nevir tidandis to them so light;   710
The kinge hym kissyd and knight and swayne.

To a chamber the kynge hym lad,
Feyre in armys they gon hym fold,
96V   And sette hym on a riche bedde
That sprad was with a clothe of gold.   715
To serve hym was there no man sad,
Ne dight hym as hymself wold
To make hym bothe blithe and glad;
And sithe auntres he them told.

Thre dayes in courte he dwellid there   720

That he ne spake not with the quene,
So myche prees was ay hym nere,
The kyng hym lad and courte bydene.
The lady bright as blossom on brere,
Sore she longid hym to sene,   725
Wepinge was hyr moste chere,
Thoughe she ne durste hyr to no man mene.

Than it felle uppon a day,
The kinge gan on huntynge ride
Into the foreste hym to playe,   730
With his knightis be his syde.
Launcelot longe in bed laye,
With the quene he thought to byde.
To the chamber he toke the way,
And salues hyr with mekell pryde.   735

Friste he kissyd that lady shene,
And salues hyr with herte fre,
And sithe the ladyes all bydene;
For joye the teres ranne on ther ble.
"Well-away," than sayd the quene,   740
"Launcelot that I evyr the se.
The love þat hathe be us bytwene,
That it shall thus departed be.

Allas, Launcelot du Lake,
Sithe thou hast all my hert in wold,   745
Th'erlis doughter that thou wold take
Off Ascalot, as men me told;
Now thou leviste for hyr sake
Alle thy dede of armys bold.
I may wofully wepe and wake,   750
In clay tylle I be clongyn cold.

But, Launcelot, I beseche the here,
Sithe it nedelyngis shall be so,

97R

That thou nevir more dyskere
The love that hathe bene betwyxe us two, 755
Ne that she nevir be with the so dere
Dede of armys þat thou be fro;
That I may of thy body here,
Sithe I shalle thus beleve in woo."

Launcelot fulle stille than stode; 760
His herte was hevy as any stone,
So sory he wexe in his mode
For routhe hym thought it all totorne.
"Madame," he said, "for crosse and rode,
What bytokenyth all this mone? 765
By Hym þat bought me with His blode,
Off these tydandes know I none.

But by these wordis thynkith me
Away ye wold þat I ware.
Now have good day, my lady fre, 770
For sothe thou seest me nevir mare."
Oute of the chambyr þan wendis he,
Now whethir his hert was full of care.
The lady swownyd sithes thre;
Almost she slew hyrselfe thare. 775

Launcelot to his chambyr yede,
There his owne atyre in lay;
Armyd hym in a noble wede.
Thoughe in his hert were litell play
Forthe he spronge as sparke of glede; 780
Withe sory chere, for sothe to say,
Up he worthis uppon his stede,
And to a foreste he wendis away.

97V Tithyngis come into the halle
That Launcelot was uppon his stede; 785
Oute than ran the knightis alle,

Off there witte as they wold wede.
Boerte de Gawnes and Lyonelle
And Ector, that doughty was of dede,
Folowyn hym on horsys snelle; 790
Fulle lowde gonne they blowe and grede.

There might no man hym ovirtake;
He rode into a forest grene.
Moche mone gonne they make,
The knightis that were bold and kene, 795
"Allas," they sayd, "Launcelot du Lake,
That evyr shuldistow se the quene."
And hyr they cursyd for his sake,
That evyr love was them bytwene.

They ne wiste nevir where to fare 800
Ne to what land þat he wold.
Ageyne they went with sighyng sare,
The knightis þat were kene and bold.
The quene they found in swownyng thare,
Hyr comely tresses all unfold, 805
They were so full of sorowe and care;
There was none hyr comfort wold.

The kynge than hastis hym for his sake,
And home þan come that ylke day,
And asked after Launcelot du Lake, 810
And they sayd he is gone away.
The quene was in hyr bed all nakyd,
And sore seke in hyr chambyr lay.
So moche mone the kynge gon make,
There was no knight þat lust to playe. 815

The kinge klepis Gawayne þat day
And alle his sorow told hym tylle,
98R   "Now ys Launcelot gone away,
And come I wote he nevir wille."

He sayd, "Allas and well-away,"   820
Sighed sore and gaff hym ylle,
"The lord that we have lovid allway,
In courte why nylle he nevir dwelle?"

Gawayn spekis in that tyde,
And to the kynge sayd he there,   825
"Sir, in this castelle shall ye byde,
Comforte you and make good chere,
And we shall bothe go and ride
In all landis ferre and nere.
So prevely he shall hym not hyde,   830
Throughe happe that we ne shall of hym here.

Knyghtis than sought hym wide,
Off Launcelot myght they not here.
Tylle it felle uppon a tyde,
Quene Genure, bright as blossom on brere,   835
To mete is sette that ylke tyde,
And Syr Gawayne satte hyr nere,
And uppon that other syde
A Scottysshe knight þat was hyr dere.

A squyer in the courte hath thought,   840
That ylke day yif that he myght,
With a poyson þat he hath wrought
To slae Gawayne yif that he mighte.
In frute he hath it forthe brought
And sette byfore the quene bright.   845
An appille overeste lay on lofte,
There the poyson was in dighte.

For he thoughte the lady bright
Wold the beste to Gawayne bede,
But she it yaff to the Scottisshe knight,   850
For he was of an unkouth stede.
Thereof he ete a lytell wight;

98V   Off tresoun toke there no man hede.
          There he loste both mayne and might,
          And died sone as I you rede.   855

          They nyste what it myght by mene;
          But up hym sterte Syr Gawayne,
          And sithen all the courte bydene,
          And ovyr the bord they have hym drayne.
          "Well-away," than sayd the quene,   860
          "Jhesu Criste, what may I sayne.
          Certis, now will all men wene
          Myself that I the knight have slayne."

          Triacle there was anone forth brought.
          The quene wende to save his lyff,   865
          But all that myght helpe hym noght,
          For there the knight is dede as swithe.
          So grete sorow the quene than wrought,
          Grete doele it was to se and lythe.
          "Lord, suche syttes me have sought,   870
          Why ne may I nevir be blithe?"

          Knyghtis done none other myght,
          Bot beryed hym with doele inoughe
          At a chapell with riche lyghte
          In a foreste by a cloughe.   875
          A riche toumbe they dyd bydight;
          A crafty clerke the lettres droughe,
          How there lay the Shottysshe knyght
          That Quene Genure with poyson slough.

          Aftyr thys a tyme byfelle,   880
          To the courte ther come a knyght,
          Hys brodyr he was, as I you telle,
          And Syr Mador for sothe he highte.
          He was an hardy man and snelle
          In turnamente and eke in fight,   885

And mykell lovyd in courte to duelle,
99R   For he was man of myche myght.

Than it felle uppon a day,
Sir Mador wente with mekill pride
Into the foreste hym for to play,   890
That floured was and braunchid wyde.
He found a chapell in his way
As he cam by a cloughis syde,
There his owne brodyr lay,
And there at Masse he thought to abyde.   895

A riche toumbe he found there dight
With lettres that were fayre inoughe;
A while he stode and redde it right.
Grete sorow than to his herte droughe:
He found the name of the Scottysshe knight   900
That Quene Genure with poysoun sloughe.
There he loste bothe mayne and myght,
And ovyr the toumbe he felle in swoughe.

Off swownynge whan he myght awake,
His herte was hevy as any lede.   905
He sighed for his brothers sake;
He ne wiste what was beste rede.
The way to courte gan he take,
Off nothinge ne stode he drede,
A loude crye on the quene gonne make   910
In chalengynge of his brothers dede.

The kynge fulle sore than gan hym drede,
For he myght not be ageyne the right;
The quene of witte wold nyghe wede,
Thoughe þat she agilte had no wight.   915
She moste there byknow the dede
Or fynde a man for hyr to fight,
For welle she wiste to deth she yede
Yif she were on a queste of knightis.

99V Thoughe Arthur were kynge þe land to weld, 920
He myght not be agayne the righte.
A day he toke with spere and sheld
To fynd a man for hyr to fight,
That she shalle eyther to deth hyr yeld
Or putte hyr on a queste of knightis; 925
Thereto bothe there handis upheld
And trewly there trouthis plighte.

Whan they in certeyne had sette a day,
And that quarelle undirtake,
The word sprange sone throw eche contrey 930
What sorow that Quene Genure ganne make.
So at the laste, shortely to say,
Word come to Launcelot du Lake
There as he seke iwoundyd lay,
Men told hym holly all the wrake, 935

How that Quene Genure the bright
Had slayne with grete treasoun
A swithe noble Scottisshe knight
At the mete with stronge poysoun.
Therefor a day was taken right 940
That she shuld fynd a knight full bowne
For hyr sake for to fighte,
Or ellis be brente withoute raunsowne.

Whan þat Launcelot du Lake
Had herd holly all this fare, 945
Grete sorow gon he to hym take
For the quene was in suche care,
And swore to venge hyr of that wrake
That day yif þat he lyvand ware.
Than payned he hym his sorows to slake 950
And wexe as breme as any bare.

100R Now leve we Launcelot there he was

Withe the ermyte in the forest grene,
And telle we forthe of the case
That touchith Arthur the kynge so kene.   955
Sir Gawayne on the morne to conselle he tase,
And mornyd sore for the quene;
Into a toure than he hym has
And ordeyned the beste there them bytwene.

And as they in there talkynge stode,   960
To ordeyne how it beste myght be,
A feyre ryver undyr the toure yode,
And sone therein gonne they see
A lytelle bote of shappe full good
To-theyme-ward with the streme gon te.   965
There myght none feyrer sayle on flode,
Ne better forgid as of tree.

Whan Kynge Arthur saw þat sighte,
He wondrid of the riche apparrayle
That was aboute the bote idighte.   970
So richely was it coveryd, sanz fayle,
In maner of a voute with clothis idighte,
Alle shynand as gold as yt ganne sayle.
Than sayd Syr Gawayne the good knight,
"This bote is of a ryche entayle."   975

"For sothe, syr," sayd the kynge tho,
"Suche one sawgh I nevyr are.
Thedir I rede now þat we go;
Som aventures shalle we se thare.
And yif it be within dight so   980
As withoute, or gayer mare,
I darre savely say, therto
Bygynne wille auntres or ought yare."

Oute of the toure adowne they wente,
The Kynge Arthur and Syr Gawayne,   985

100V

To the bote they yede withoute stynte,
They two allone, for sothe to sayne,
And whan they come there as it lente,
They byheld it faste, is not to layne.
A clothe that over the bote was bente   990
Sir Gawayne lyfte up, and went in bayne.

Whan they were in, withouten lese,
Ful richely arayed they it found,
And in the myddis a feyre bedde was
For any kynge of Cristene lond.   995
Than as swithe or they wold sese
The koverlet lyfte they up with hand,
A dede woman they sighe ther was,
The fayrest mayde þat myght be found.

To Sir Gawayne than sayd the kynge,   1000
"For sothe, dethe was to unhende
Whan he wold thus fayre a thinge
Thus yonge oute of the world do wend.
For hyr biaute, withoute lesynge,
I wold fayne wete of hyr kynd,   1005
What she was, this swete derelynge,
And in hyr lyff where she gonne lend."

Sir Gawayne his eyen than on hyr caste,
And byheld hyr fast with herte fre,
So that he knew welle at the laste   1010
That the mayde of Ascalote was she,
Whiche he som tyme had wowyd faste
His owne leman for to be.
But she aunsweryd hym ay in haste,
To none bot Launcelot wold she te.   1015

To the kinge þan sayd Sir Gawayne tho,
"Thinke ye not on this endris day,
Whan my lady the quene and we two

Stode togedir in youre play,
Off a mayde I told you tho   1020
That Launcelot lovyd paramoure ay."
"Gawayne, for sothe," the kynge sayd tho,

"Whan thou it saydiste wele thinke I may."

"For sothe, syr," þan sayd Sir Gawayne,
"This is the mayd that I of spake.   1025
Most in this world, is not to layne,
She lovid Launcelot du Lake."
"For sothe," the kynge þan gon to sayne,
"Me rewith the deth of hyr for his sake;
The inchesoun wold I wete full fayne,   1030
For sorow I trow deth gon hyr take."

Than Sir Gawayne the good knight
Sought about hyr withoute stynte,
And found a purs fulle riche arighte
With gold and perlis þat was ibente,   1035
All empty semyd it noght to sight.
That purs full sone in hond he hente;
A letter thereof than oute he twight,
Than wete they wold fayne what it mente.

What there was wreten wete they wold,   1040
And Sir Gawayn it toke the kynge
And bad hym open yt that he shold.
So dyd he sone, withoute lesynge,
Than found he whan it was unfold
Bothe the ende and the bygynnynge.   1045
Thus was it wreten, as men me told,
Off that fayre maydens deynge.

"To Kynge Arthur and all his knightis
That longe to the Round Table,
That corteyse bene and most of myghtis,   1050
Doughty and noble, trew and stable,

And most worshipfull in all fyghtis,
To the nedefull helpinge and profitable,
The mayde of Ascalot to rightis
Sendith gretinge withouten fable: 1055

To you all, my playnte I make
Off the wronge that me is wroghte,
But noght in maner to undirtake
That any of you shold mend it ought,
Bot onely I say for this sake   1060
That thoughe this world were throw sought,
Men shold nowhere fynd your make,
All noblisse to fynde that myght be sought.

Therefore to you to undirstand
That for I trewly many a day   1065
Have lovid lelyest in lond,
Dethe hathe me fette of this world away.
To wete for whome yif ye will found
That I so longe for in langoure lay,
To say the sothe wille I noght wound,   1070
For gaynes it not for to say nay.

To say you the sothe tale
For whome I have suffred this woo,
I say deth hathe me take with bale
For the noblest knight þat may go: 1075
Is none so doughty dyntis to dale,
So ryalle ne so fayre therto,
But so churlysshe of maners in feld ne hale
Ne know I none of frende ne fo.

Off foo ne frend, the sothe to say,   1080
So unhend of thewis is ther none,
His gentillnesse was all away,
All churlysshe maners he had in wone
For for nothinge þat I coude pray,

Knelynge ne wepinge with rewfull mone,   1085
To be my leman he sayd evyr nay
And sayd shortely he wold have none.

Forthy lordis, for his sake,
I toke to herte grete sorow and care;
So at the laste, deth gonne me take,   1090
So þat I might lyve na mare.

102R   For trew lovynge had I suche wrake
And was of blysse ibrowghte all bare;
All was for Launcelote du Lake
To wete wisely for whom it ware."   1095

When that Arthure the noble kyng
Had redde the letter and kene the name,
He said to Gawayne withoute lesynge
That Launcelott was gretly to blame,
And had hym wonne a reproovyng   1100
Forevyr, and a wikkyd fame,
Sythe she deide for grete lovyng
That he her refusyd, it may hym shame.

To the kyng than sayd Syr Gawayne,
"I gabbyd on hym thys ʒendyr day   1105
That he longede whan I gon sayne
With lady other with som othyr maye.
Bot sothe than sayde ye, is not to layne,
That he nolde nought hys love laye
In so low a place in vayne,   1110
But on a pryse lady and a gaye."

"Syr Gawayne," sayd the kyng thoo,
"What is now thy best rede,
How mow we with thys maydyn do?"
Syr Gawayne sayd, "So God me spede,   1115
Iff that ye wille assent therto,
Worshippffully we shulle hyr lede

Into the palys and bery her so
As fallys a dukys doughter in dede."

Therto the kyng assentid sone.   1120
Syr Gawayne dyd men sone be ȝare,
And worshippfully as well to done,
Into the palyse they her bare.
The kyng than tolde without lone
To all hys barons lesse and mare   1125
How Launcelot nolde noughte graunte hyr bone,
Therfore she dyed for sorow and care.

To the quene than went Syr Gawayne,
And gon to tell hyr all the case,
"For sothe, madame," he gon to sayne,   1130
"I yelde me gyllty of a trespas.
I gabbyd on Launcelot, is not to layne,
Of that I tolde yow in thys place.
I sayde that hys bydyng bayne
The Dukys doughter of Ascolote was.   1135

102V   Off Ascalot that mayden fre,
I sayd you she was hys leman.
That I so gabbyd it rewith me,
For all the sothe now telle I can:
He nold hyr nought we mowe welle se,   1140
Forthy dede is that white as swanne,
Thys lettere thereof waraunte wolle be:
She playnethe on Launcelot to eche man."

The quene was as wrothe as wynde,
And to Syr Gawayne sayd she than,   1145
"For sothe, Syr, thou were to unkynde
To gabbe so uppon any man,
But thou haddyst wist the sothe in mynde
Whether that it were sothe ore nan.
Thy curtessy was all behynde   1150
Whan thou thoo sawes freste began.

Thy worshippe thou undediste gretlyche
Suche wronge to wite that good knyght.
I trowe he ne agulte the nevyr nought myche,
Why that thou oughtiste with no ryghte   1155
To gabbe on hym so wylanlyche
Thus behynde hym oute of hys syghte.
And, syr, thou ne woste not ryght wiseliche
What harme hathe falle thereof and myght.

I wende thou haddiste be stable and trewe   1160
And full of all curtessye,
Bot now me thynke thy maners newe,
Thay bene all tornyd to vilanye;
Now thou on knyghtis makeste thy glewe,
To lye uppon hem for envye.   1165
Who that the worshippeth it may hem rewe;
Therefore devoyede my companye."

Syr Gawayne than slyghly wente awaye,
He syghe the quene agrevyd sore.
No more to hyr than wolde he saye,   1170
Bot trowyd hyr wrathe have evyr more.
The quene than, as she nyghe wode were,
Wryngyd hyr handys and said, "Well-awaye,
Allas in world that I was bore,
That I am a wreche welle say I may.   1175

Herte, allas, why were thou wode,
To trowe that Launcelot du Lake
Were so falsse and fykelle of mode
Another lemman than the to take.
Nay, sertes, for alle thys worldis goode,   1180
He nolde to me have wrought suche wrake."

103R   To fynde a man for hyr to feyghte   1318

Or elles yeld her to be brente.
Iff she were on a quest of knyghtis,   1320
Wele sche wiste she shold be shente;
Thoughe that she agilte hade no wight,
No lenger lyffe myght hyr be lente.

The kynge than sighed and gaffe hym ylle,
And to Syr Gawayne than he yede,   1325
To Bors de Gawnes and Lyonelle,
To Estor, that doughty was in dede,
And askyd yif eny were in wille
To helpe hym in that mykyll nede.
The quene one knes before hem felle,   1330
That neyghe oute of hyr wite she yede.

The knyghtes answeryd with lytell pride,
Her hertes was full of sorow and woughe,
Sayd, "All we saughe and satte besyde
The knyght when she with poyson sloughe;   1335
And sythe in herte is nought to hyde,
Syr Gawayne over the bord hym droughe.
Agayne the ryght we wille not ryde:
We saw the sothe verely inoughe."

The quene wepte and sighed sore,   1340
To Bors de Gawnes went she thoo,
On knes byfore hym fell she thore
That nyghe her hert braste in two,
"Lord Bors," she seyde, "thyn ore,
Today I shall to dethe goo   1345
Bot yiffe thy worthy wylle wore
To brynge my lyffe oute of thys woo."

Bors de Gawnes stille stode
And wrothe away hys yȝen wente,
"Madame," he sayde, "by crosse on rode,   1350
Thou art wele worthy to be brente.

The nobleste bodye of flesshe and blode
That evyr was yete in erthe lente
For thy wille and thy wykkyd mode
Out of oure companye is wente."　　　　　　1355

Than she wepte and gaffe hyr ille,
And to Syr Gawayne than she yede,
On knes downe before hym felle,
That neigh oute of hyr witte she yede,
"Mercy," she cryed loude and shrylle,　　　　1360
"Lord, as I no gilt have of thys dede,
Yif it were thy worthy wille
Today to helpe me in thys nede."

Gawayne answeryd with litelle pride,
Hys hert was full of sorow and woughe,　　　1365
"Dame, saw I not and sat besyde
The knyght whan thou with poyson sloughe;
And sythe in hert is not to hyde,
Myselfe over the bord hym droughe.
Agayne the ryght wille I not ryde:　　　　　1370
I sawghe the sothe verrye inoughe."

Than she wente to Lyonelle,
That ever had bene her owne knyght,
On knes downe before hym felle
That neyghe she lost mayne and myght,　　　1375
"Mercy", she cryed loude and shrylle,
"Lord, as I ne have gilte no wyght,
Yif it were thy worthy wylle
For my lyffe to take thys fyght."

"Madame, how may thou to us take　　　　　1380
And wote thyselfe so wytterly
That thou hast Launcelot du Lake
Brought oute of ower companye.
We may syghe and monynge make

103V

Whan we se knyghtis kene in crye;   1385
Be Hym thatt me to man gan shape,
We ar glade that thou it abye."

Than full sore she gan hyr drede,
Welle she wiste hyr lyffe was lorne;
Loude gon she wepe and grede,   1390
And Estor kneles she beforne:
"For Hym that on the rode gon sprede
And for us bare the crone of thorne,
Estor helpe now in thys nede
Or certes today my lyfe is lorne."   1395

"Madame, how may thou to us take,
Or how sholde I for the feyght;
Take the now Launcelot du Lake,
That evyr has bene thyn owne knyght.
My dere brother for thy sake   1400
I ne shall hym nevyr se with sight.
Cursyde be he that the batalle take
To save thy lyffe agayne the ryghte."

Ther wolde no man the batayle take;
The quene wente to her chambyr soo,   1405
So dulefully mone gon she make
That nyghe hyr hert brast in twoo.
For sorow gon she shever and quake,
And sayd, "Allas, and wele-a-woo,
Why nade I now Launcelot du Lake,   1410
All the curte nolde me noght sloo.

Yvelle have I besette the dede
That I have worshipped so many a knyght,
And I have no man in my nede   1413A
For my lyffe darre take fight.
Lord kynge of all thede,   1415
That all the worlde shall rede and ryght,

Launcelot thou save and hede
Sithe I ne shalle nevyr hym se with syght."

The quene wepte and gave hyr ylle;
Whan she sawe the fyre was yare,　　　　1420
Than mornyd she full stille.
To Bors de Gawnys went sho thare,
Bysought hym yif it were hys wille
To helpe hyr in hyr mekylle care.
In swounynge she before hym felle　　　　1425
That wordys myght sho speke no mare.

Whan Bors saw the quene so bryght,
Of her he hade grete pyte;
In hys armys he helde her upe-ryght,
Bade hyr of good comfort be,　　　　1430
"Madame, but there come a better knyght
That wolde the bataile take for the,
I shalle myselve for the fighte
Whyle any lyffe may laste in me."

Than was the quene wonder blythe　　　　1435
That Bors de Gawnys wolde for her feyght
That nere for joye she swounyd swythe,
But as that he her helde upryght.
To hyr chambre he led hyr blythe,
To ladyes and to maydens bryght,　　　　1440
And bad she shulde it to no man kythe
Tylle he were armyd and redy dyght.

Bors, that was bolde and kene,
Clepyd all hys other knyghtis,
And tokyn conselle hem betwene,　　　　1445
The beste that thay couthe and myght,
How that he hathe hyght the quene
That ilke day for hyr to feyght
Ayenste Syr Mador full of tene,
To save hyr lyfe yife that he myght.　　　　1450

104V

The knyghtis answerd with wo and wrake,
And sayd they wyste wetterlye
That "she hathe Launcelot du Lake
Browght oute of ouere companye.
Nys non that nolde thys bataile take   1455
Er she hade any vylanye,
But we nylle not so glad hyr make
Byfore we ne suffre hyr to be sorye."

Bors and Lionelle the knyght,
Estor, that doughty was of dede,   1460
To the forest than went thay ryght,
There orysons at the chapelle to bede
To Oure Lord God all full of myght
That day sholde lene hem wele to spede,
A grace to venquesshe the feyght;   1465
Of Syr Mador thay hade grete drede.

As they came by the forest syde,
There orysons for to make,
The nobleste knyght than saue thay ryde
That ever was in erthe shape.   1470
Hys loreme lemyd all with pride,
Stede and armure all was blake;
Hys name is noght to hele and hyde,
He hyght Syr Launcelot du Lake.

What wondyr was thoughe they were blythe   1475
Whan they ther mayster se with syght,
On knes felle thay as swythe,
And thankyd all to God Allmyght.
Joye it was to here and lythe
The metynge of the noble knyght,   1480
And after he askid also swythe,
"How now farys my lady bryght?"

Bors than tolde hym all the ryght,

105R

It was no lenger for to hyde,
How there dyed a Scottysche knyght   1485
Atte the mete the quene besyde.
"Today, syr, is here dethe all dyght,
It may no lenger be to byde,
And I for hyr have take the feyght."

"Syr Mador, stronge though that he be,   1490
I hope he shall welle prove hys myght.
To the courte now wende ye thre
And recoumforte my lady bryghte,
Bot loke ye speke no word of me;
I wolle come as a strange knyght."   1495

Launcelot that was mochelle of myght
Abydys in the forest grene;
To the courte wente these othyr knyghtis
For to recomforte the quene.
To make hyr glade with all theyre myght,   1500
Grete joye they made hem bytwene.
Forwhy she ne sholde drede no wyght,
Off goode comforte they bade her bene.

Bordes were sette and clothys sprede;
The kyng hymselfe is gone to sytte;   1505
The quene is to the table lade
With chekys that were wanne and wete.
Off sorow were they nevyr unsad,
Myght they neyther drynke ne ete.
The quene of dethe was sore adrade   1510
That grymly terys gone she lete.

And as thay were at the thryd mese,
The kynge and all the courte bedene,
Syr Mador all redy was,
With helme and shelde and haubarke shene.   1515
Amonge hem all before the dese,

He blowith oute uppon the quene
To have hys ryght withouten lese,
As were the covenantes hem bytwene.

The kyng lokyde one all hys knyghtis,   1520
Was he nevere yet so woo;
Saw he nevyr on hym dyght
105V   Ayenste Syr Mador for to goo.
Syr Mador swore by Goddys myght
As he was man of herte thro,   1525
Bot yif he hastely have hys ryght,
Amonge hem all he sholde hyr slo.

Than spake the kynge of mekelle myght,
That ay was cortayse and hende,
"Syr, lete us ete and sythen us dyght;   1530
Thys day nys nought yit gone to the ende,
Yet myght there come suche a knyght,
Yif Goddys wyll were hym to sende,
To fynde the thy fylle of fyghte
Or the sonne to grounde wende."   1535

Bors than loughe on Lyonelle,
Wyste no man of here hertys worde.
Hys chambyr anone he wendys tylle
Withoute any othyr worde,
Armyd hym at all hys wille   1540
With helme and haubarke, spere and sworde.
Agayne than comys he full stylle
And sette hym downe to the borde.

The terys ranne on the kyngis ble
For joye that he sawe Bors adyght.   1545
Up he rose with herte free,
And Bors in armys clyppis ryght,
And sayd, "Bors, God foryelde it the
In thys nede that thow wolde fyghte;

Welle acquyteste thou it me 1550
That I have worshipped any knyght."

Than as Syr Mador loudeste spake
The quene of treson to bycalle,
Comys Syr Launcelot du Lake,
Rydand ryght into the halle. 1555
Hys stede and armure all was blake,
Hys visere over hys yȝen falle;
Many a man bygonne to quake,
Adrade of hym nyghe were they alle.

Then spake the kynge mykelle of myght, 1560
That hend was in iche a sythe,
"Syr, is it youre wille to lyghte,
Ete and drynke and make you blythe?"
Launcelot spake as a strange knyght,
106R "Nay, Syr," he sayd as swythe, 1565
"I herde telle here of a fight,
I come to save a ladyes lyve.

Yevell hathe the quene bysette hyr dedys
That she hathe worsshippid many a knyght,
And she hathe no man in her nedys 1570
That for hyr lyfe dare take a fight.
Thou that hyr of treson gredys,
Hastely that thow be dyghte,
Oute of thy witte þoughe that thou wedis,
Today thou shalt prove all thy myght." 1575

Than was Syr Mador also blythe
As foule of day after the nyght,
To hys stede he wente that sythe
As man that was of moche myght.
To the felde than ryde thay swythe, 1580
Hem folowes bothe kyng and knyght
The bataile for to se and lythe;
Saugh nevir no man a stronger fyght.

Unhorsid were bothe knyghtis kene,
They metten with so myche mayne, 1585
And sythe thay faught with swerdys kene,
Bothe on fote. For sothe to sayne,
In alle the batailles that Launcelot had bene
With hard acountres hym agayne,
In poynte hade he nevir bene 1590
So nyghehande for to have be slayne.

There was so wondyr stronge a fyghte,
O fote nolde nouther fle ne founde
Frome loughe none tylle late nyght,
Bot gyffen many a wofull wounde. 1595
Launcelot than gaffe a dynte with myght,
Syr Mador fallys at laste to grounde.
"Mercy," cryes that noble knyght,
Fore he was seke and sore unsound.

Thoughe Launcelot were breme as bore, 1600
Full stournely he ganne upstande;
O dynte wolde he smyte no more,
Hys swerd he threwe oute of hys hande.
106V Syr Mador by God than sware,
"I have foughte in many a lande, 1605
With knyghtis bothe lesse and mare,
And nevyr yit er my mache I founde.

Bot, Syr, a prayer I wolde make
For thynge that ye love moste on lyfe,
And for oure swete Lady sake, 1610
Youer name that ye wolde me kythe."
Launcelot gan hys viser up take,
And hendely hym shewed that sythe.
Whan he saughe Launcelot du Lake,
Was nevyr man on molde so blythe. 1615

"Lord," thane said he, "welle is me,

Myne avauntement that I may make
That I have stande on dynte of the,
And foughten with Launcelot du Lake.
My brothers dethe forgeffen be   1620
To the quene for thy sake."
Launcelot hym kyste with herte fre,
And in hys armys gan hym up take.

Kynge Arthur than loude spake,
Amonge hys knyghtis to the quene,   1625
"Za, yonder is Launcelot du Lake,
Yiff I hym evyr with syght have sene."
Thay ryden and ronne than for hys sake,
The kynge and alle hys knyghtis kene;
In hys armys he gon hym take,   1630
The kynge hym kyste and courte bydene.

Than was the quene glade inoghe
Whan she saw Launcelot du Lake
That nyghe for joy she felle in swoughe,
Bot as the lordys hyr gan up take.   1635
The knyghtis all wepte and loughe
For joye as thay togedyr spake;
Withe Syr Mador withouten woughe
Full sone acordement gon they make.

It was no lenger for to abyde,   1640
Bot to the castelle thay rode as swythe
Withe trompys and with mykelle pryde
That joy it was to here and lythe.
Thoughe Syr Mador myght not go ne ryde,
To the curte is he brought that sythe,   1645
107R   And knyghtis uppon iche a syde
To make hym bothe glad and blythe.

The squeers than were takyn alle,
And thay ar put in harde payne,

Whiche that servyd in the halle   1650
Whan the knyght was with poyson slayne.
There he grauntyd amonge hem alle,
It myght no lenger be to layne,
How in an appelle he dede the galle
And hadde it thought to Syr Gawayne.   1655

Whan Syr Mador herde all the ryght,
That no gylte hadde the lady shene,
For sorowe he loste mayne and myghte,
And on knees felle before the quene.
Launcelot then hym helde uppe-ryghte   1660
For love that was them betwene;
Hym kyste bothe kynge and knyght
And sythen all the curte bydene.

The squyer than was done to shende,
As it was bothe lawe and ryght,   1665
Drawen and hongyd and forbrende
Before Syr Mador, the noble knyghte.
In the castelle thay gan forthe lende,
The Joyus Gard than was it hyghte.
Launcelot that was so hende,   1670
Thay honouryd hym with alle ther myght.

A tyme befelle, sothe to sayne,
The knyghtis stode in chambyr and spake,
Bothe Gaheriet and Syr Gawayne
And Mordreite, that mykelle couthe of wrake. 1675
"Allas", than sayde Syr Agrawayne,
"How fals men schalle we us make,
And how longe shalle we hele and layne
The treson of Launcelote du Lake?

Wele we wote withouten wene,   1680
The Kynge Arthur oure eme sholde be,
And Launcelote lyes by the quene.

Ageyne the kynge trator is he,
And that wote all the curte bydene,
And iche day it here and see.   1685
To the kynge we shulde it mene,
Yif ye wille do by the counselle of me."

107V

"Wele wote we," sayd Syr Gawayne,
"That we ar of the kyngis kynne;
And Launcelot is so mykyll of mayne   1690
That suche wordys were better blynne.
Welle wote thou, brothyr Agrawayne,
Thereof shulde we bot harmys wynne;
Yit were it better to hele and layne
Than werre and wrake thus to begynne.   1695

Welle wote thow, brother Agrawayne,
Launcelot is hardy knyght and thro.
Kynge and courte hade ofte bene slayne
Nad he bene better than we mo,
And sythen myght I nevyr sayne   1700
The love that has bene bytwene us twoo.
Launcelot shalle I nevyr betrayne,
Byhynde hys bake to be hys foo.

Launcelot is kynges sonne full good,
And therto hardy knyght and bolde,   1705
And sythen and hym ned bystode,
Many a lande wolde with hym holde.
Shedde ther sholde be mykelle blode
For thys tale, yiffe it were tolde.
Syr Agrawayne, he were full wode   1710
That suche a thynge begynne wolde."

Than thus gatys as the knyghtis stode,
Gawayne and all that other pres,
In come the kynge with mylde mode.
Gawayne than sayd, "Felaus, pees."   1715

The kynge for wrathe was neghe wode
For to wette what it was;
Aggrawayne swore by crosse and rode,
"I shalle it you telle withoute lees."

Gawayne to hys chambyr wente,   1720
Off thys tale nolde he noght here.
Gaheriet and Gaheryes of hys asente
Withe here brother went they there;
Welle they wyste that all was shente.
And Syr Gawayne by God than swere,   1725
"Here now is made a comsemente
That bethe not fynysshyd many a yere."

Syr Agrawayne tolde alle bedene
To the kynge with symple chere,
How Launcelot liggys by the quene,   1730
And so has done full many a yere,
And that wote all the courte bydene,
And iche day it se and here,
And "we have false and treytours bene
That we ne wolde nevyr to you dyskere."   1735

"Allas," than sayd the kynge thore,
"Certes that were grete pyte.
So as man nad nevyr yit more
Off biaute ne of bounte,
Ne man in worlde was nevyr yit more   1740
Off so mykylle noblyte.
Allas, full grete duelle it were
In hym shulde any treson be.

But sythe it is so, withouten fayle,
Syr Agrawayne, so God the rede,   1745
What were now thy beste consayle
For to take hym with the dede.
He is man of suche apparayle

108R

Off hym I have full mychelle drede:
All the courte nolde hym assayle 1750
Yiff he were armyd uppon hys stede."

"Syr, ye and all the courte bydene
Wendythe tomorowe on huntynge ryght,
And sythen send word to the quene
That ye wille dwelle withoute all nyght, 1755
And I and other twelve knyghtes kene,
Full prevely we shall us dyght,
We shalle hym have withouten wene
Tomorow, or any day by lyght."

On the morow with all the courte bydene, 1760
The kynge gonne on huntynge ryde,
And sythen he sent word to the quene
That he wolde all nyght oute abyde.
Aggrawayne with twelve knyghtys kene
Atte home be lefte that ilke tyde, 1765
Off alle the day they were not sene
So prewely thay gonne hem hyde.

Tho was the quene wondyr blythe
That the kynge wolde at the foreste dwelle,
To Launcelot she sente as swythe, 1770
And bad that he shulde come her tille.
Syr Bors de Gawnes beganne to lythe,
108V Thoughe hys herte lyked ille,
"Syr," he said, "I wolde you kythe
A word yif that it were your wille. 1775

Syr, tonyght I rede ye dwelle,
I drede ther be som treson dight
Withe Agrawayne that is so felle,
That waites you bothe day and nyght.
Off alle that ye have gonne hyr tylle, 1780
Ne grevyd me nevyr yit no wight,

Ne nevyr yit gaffe myn herte to ille,
So mykelle as it dothe tonyght."

"Bors," he sayd, "holde stylle,
Suche wordys ar noughte to kythe.   1785
I wille wende my lady tille
Som new tythandes for to lythe.
I ne shall nought bote wete hyr wylle;
Loke ye make youe glad and blythe.
Certenly, I nelle nought dwelle,   1790
Bot come agayne to youe all swythe."

Forwhy he wende have comynne sone,
For to dwelle had he not thought.
Non armore he dyde hym uppon,
Bot a robe all sengle wrought;   1795
In hys hand a swerd he fone,
Off tresson dred he hym ryght noght;
There was no man undyr the mone
He wende with harme durste hym haffe sought.

Whan he come to the lady shene,   1800
He kissid and clypped that swete wyght;
For sothe they nevyr wolde wene
That any treson was ther dyght.
So mykylle love was hem bytwene
That they noght departe myght;   1805
To bede he gothe with the quene
And there he thoughte to dwelle alle nyght.

He was not buskyd in hys bedde,
Launcelot in the quenys boure,
Come Agrawayne and Syr Mordreit   1810
With twelve knyghtys stiffe in stowre.
Launcelot of tresson they begredde,
Callyd hym fals and kyngys treytoure;
And he so strongly was bystedde,
Thereinne he hadde non armoure.   1815

109R   "Wel-away," than sayd the quene,
"Launcelot, what shall worthe of us twoo?
The love that hathe bene us betwene
To suche endynge that it sholde goo,
Withe Agrawayne that is so kene,   1820
That nyght and day hathe bene oure foo.
Now I wote withouten wene,
That alle oure wele is tornyd to woo."

"Lady," he sayd, "thow moste blynne,
Wyde I wote thes wordis bethe ryffe.   1825
Bot is here any armoure inne
That I may have to save my lyffe?"
"Certis, nay," she sayd thenne,
"Thys antoure is so wondyr stryffe,
That I ne may to none armoure wynne,   1830
Helme ne hauberke, swerd ne knyffe."

Evyr Agrawayne and Syr Mordred
Callyd hym recreante fals knyght,
Bad hym ryse oute of hys bedde,
For he moste nedis with them fyght.   1835
In hys robe than he hym cled,
Thoughe he none armoure gete myght,
Wrothely oute hys swerd he bredde;
The chamber dore he sette upryght.

An armyd knyght before in wente   1840
And wende Launcelot wele to sloo,
Bot Launcelot gaffe hym soche a dynte
That to the grounde gonne he go.
The other all agayne than stente,
Aftyr hym dorste folowe no moo;   1845
To the chambyr dore he sprente
And claspid it with barres twoo.

The knyght that Launcelot has slayne,

Hys armoure founde he fayre and bryght;
Hastely he hathe hem of drayne 1850
And therin hymselfe dight.
"Now know thou wele, Syr Agrawayne,
Thow presons me no more tonyght."
Oute than sprange he with mykell mayn,
Hymselfe ayenste hem alle to fyght. 1855

Launcelot than smote with herte goode;
Wete ye welle withouten lese,
Syr Agrawayne to dethe yode
And sythen all the other presse.
Was non so stronge that hym withstode, 1860
Be he had made a lytelle rese.
Bot Mordreit fled as he were wode,
To save hys lyff full fayne he was.

Launcelot to hys chambre yode,
To Bors and to hys other knyghtis. 1865
Bors armyd before hym stode,
To bedde yit was he noȝt dight.
The knyghtis for fere was nye wode,
So were they drechyd all that nyght,
Bot blythe wexid they in her mode 1870
Whan they her mastyr sawghe with syght.

"Syr," sayd Bors, the hardy knyght,
"Aftyr you have we thoght full longe,
To bedde durste I me noȝt dight
For drede ye hade som aunter stronge. 1875
Owre knyghtis have be drechyd tonyght
That som nakyd oute of bed spronge,
Forthy we were full sore afryght
Leste som treson were us amonge."

"Ya, Bors, drede the no wight, 1880
Bot bethe of herte good and bolde,

109V

And swythe awaken up all my knyghtis,
And loke whiche wille with us holde.
Loke they be armyd and redy dight,
For it is sothe that thou me tolde,   1885
We have begonne thys ilke nyght
That shall brynge many a man full colde."

Bors than spake with drery mode,
"Syr," he sayd, "sithe it is so,
We shalle be of hertis good,   1890
Aftyr the wele to take the wo."
The knyghtis sprent as they were wode,
And to there harneise gon the go.
At the morow armyd before hym stode,
An hundrethe knyghtis and squyers mo.   1895

Whan they were armyd and redy dight,
A softe pas forthe gonne they ride
As men that were of mykelle myght
To a forest there besyde.
Launcelot arrayes all hys knyghtis,   1900
And there they loggen hem to byde
110R   Tylle they herd of the lady bryght,
What auntere of hyr shulde betyde.

Mordreit than toke away full gayne,
And to the forest wente he right;   1905
Hys auntures tolde, for sothe to sayne,
That were byfallyn that ylke nyght.
"Mordreit, have ye that treitour slayne,
Or how have ye with hym dight?"
"Nay, syr, bot dede is Aggrawayne,   1910
And so ar all oure other knyghtis."

Whan it herde Syr Gawayne
That was so hardy knyght and bolde,
"Allas, is my brother slayne?"

Sore hys herte began to colde.   1915
"I warnyd wele Syr Aggrawayne
Or evyr yit thys tale was tolde,
Launcelot was so myche of mayne
Ayenste hym was stronge to holde."

It was no lenger for to byde;   1920
Kynge and all hys knyghtis kene
Toke there counselle in that tyde
What was beste do with the quene.
It was no lenger for to byde,
That day forbrent shuld she bene.   1925

The fyre than made they in the felde;
Thereto they brought that lady fre,
All that evyr myght wepene welde,
Aboute her armyd for to bee.
Gawayne, that styffe was undir shelde,   1930
Gaheryet ne Gaheryes ne wold noȝt see;
In there chamber they hem helde,
Off hyr they had grete pyte.

The Kynge Arthure that ylke tyde
Gawayne and Gaherys for sent;   1935
Here answeres were noȝt for to hyde,
They ne wolde noȝt be of hys assente.
Gawayne wolde nevyr be nere bysyde
There any woman shuld be brente.
Gaheriet and Gaheries with lytell pryde   1940
All unarmyd thedyr they wente.

A squeer gonne tho tythandes lythe
That Launcelot to courte had sente,
To the foreste he wente as swithe
There Launcelote and hys folke was lente,   1945
110V   Bad hem come and haste blythe,
The quene is ledde to be brente.

And they to hors and armes swythe,
And iche one before other sprente.

The quene by the fyre stode   1950
And in hyr smoke allredy was;
Lordyngis was there many and good,
And grete power withouten lese.
Launcelote sprente as he were wode,
Full sone partyd he the prees,   1955
Was none so styffe aȝeynste hym stode
Be he had made a lytelle rese.

There was no stele stode hem aȝeyne,
Though faught they but a lytelle stound;
Lordyngys that were myche of mayne,   1960
Many goode were brought to grounde:
Gaheriet and Gaheries bothe were slayne
Wythe many a doulfull dethes wounde.
The quene thay toke withoute layne
And to the foreste gonne they founde.   1965

The tythyngis is to the kynge brought,
How Launcelote has tane away the quene,
"Suche wo as there is wroughte,
Slayne ar alle oure knyghtis kene."
Downe he felle and swounyd ofte,   1970
Grete duelle it was to here and sene,
So nere hys herte the sorowe sought
Allmoste hys lyffe wolde no man wene.

"Jhesu Cryste, what may I sayne?
In erthe was nevyr man so wo.   1975
Suche knyghtys as there ar slayne,
In all thys worlde there is no mo.
Lette no man telle Syr Gawayne
Gaheriet hys brother is dede hym fro.
But weil-away the reufulle rayne,   1980
That evyr Launcelote was my fo."

Gawayne gonne in hys chambyr hym holde,
Off all the day he nolde not oute goo.
A squyer than the tythandys tolde;
What wondyr theighe hys herte were wo.   1985
"Allas," he sayde, "my brother bolde,
Where Gahereit be dede me fro."
So sore hys hert began to colde,
Allmoste he wolde hymselff sloo.

The squyer spake with drery mode   1990
To recomfort Syr Gawayne,
"Gaheriet eyles noght bot goode,
He wolle sone come agayne."
Gawayne sprent as he were wode
To the chambre there they lay slayne.   1995
The chambre flore all ranne on blode,
And clothys of golde were over hem drayne.

A clothe he hevys than uppon hyght,
What wondyr thoughe hys hert were sore,
So dulfully to se them dight   2000
That ere so doughty knyghtis were.
Whan he hys brother sawghe with syght,
A word myght he speke no more;
There he loste mayne and myght,
And ovyr hym felle in swounynge thore.   2005

Off swounynge whan he myght awake,
The hardy knyght, Syr Gawayne,
Be God he sware and loude spake
As man that myche was of mayne,
"Betwixte me and Launcelote du Lake,   2010
Nys man in erthe, for sothe to sayne,
Shall trewes sette and pees make
Er outher of us have other slayne."

A squyer that Launcelot to court hadde sente,

111R

Off the tythandys gonne he lythe.   2015
To the foreste is he wente
And tolde Launcelot also swythe,
How lordynges that were riche of rente,
Fele goode had loste hyr lyffe;
Gaheryet and Gaheries sought here ende.   2020
Bot than was Launcelot nothynge blythe.

"Lord," he said, "what may thys bene?
Jhesu Cryste, what may I sayne?
The love that hathe betwexte us bene,
That evyr Gaheryet me was agayne.   2025
Now I wote for all bydene,
A sorye man is Syr Gawayne,
Acordement thar me nevyr wene

111V   Tille eyther of us have other slayne."

Launcelot gonne with hysse folke forthe wende   2030
Withe sory hert and drery mode.
To quenys and countesses fele he sende,
And grete ladyes of gentill blode,
That he had ofte here landis deffende,
And foughten whan hem nede bystode.   2035
Ichone her power hym lende,
And made hys party stiffe and goode.

Quenys and countesses that ryche were
Sende hym erlys with grete meyne,
Other ladies that myght no more   2040
Sente hym barons or knyghtis free.
So mykelle folke to hym gon fare,
Hydous it was hys oste to see.
To the Joyus Gard wente he thare,
And helde hym in that stronge cyte.   2045

Launcelotis herte was full sore
For the lady fayre and bryght;

A damosselle he dyd be yare,
In ryche apparayle was she dyght,
Hastely in message for to fare   2050
To the kynge of mykelle myght.
To prove it fals what myght he mare,
Bot proferys hym therefore to fyght.

The mayden is redy for to ryde
In a full ryche aparaylmente   2055
Off samytte grene, with mykyll pryde,
That wroght was in the oryente;
A dwerffe shulde wende by hyr syde,
Suche was Launcelotis comaundemente.
So were the manerys in that tyde   2060
Whan a mayde on message wente.

To the castelle whan she come,
In the paleise gonne she lyght.
To the kynge hyr erande she sayd sone,
By hym satte Syr Gawayne the knyght,   2065
Sayd that lyes were sayde hym uppon:
Trewe they were by day and nyght.
112R   To prove it as a knyght shulde done,
Launcelot proferis hym to fyghte.

The Kynge Arthure spekys thore   2070
Wordys that were kene and thro,
"He ne myght prove it nevir more,
Bot of my men that he wold slo."
Be Jhesu Cryste, the kynge sware,
And Syr Gawayne than also,   2075
"His dedis shall be bought full sore
Bot yife no stele nyll in hym go."

The mayden hathe hyr answere,
To the Joyus Garde gonne she ryde.
Suche as the kynges wordis were   2080

She tolde Launcelot in that tyde.
Launcelot syghed wounder sore,
Teres frome hys yȝen ganne glyde.
Bors de Gawns by Gode than sware,
"In mydde the felde we shall hem byde."   2085

Arthure wolde no lenger abyde,
Bot hastis hym with all hys myght.
Messengeres dyd he go and ryde
That thay ne shulde lette for day ne nyght,
Thorowoute Yngland by iche a syde   2090
To erle, baroun, and to knyght;
Bad hem come that ilke tyde
Withe hors stronge and armure bryght.

Thoughe the knyght that were dede hem fro,
Thereof was all there mykelle kare;   2095
Thre hundrethe thay made mo,
Oute of the castelle or they wold fare,
Off Ynglonde and Yreland also,
Off Walys and Scottis that beste were,
Launcelot and hys folkys to slo   2100
Withe hertis breme as any bore.

Whan thys oste was all bowne,
It was no lenger for to byde.
Rayses spere and gounfanoune,
As men that were of mykelle pryde.   2105
With helme and shelde and hauberke browne,
Gawayne hymselfe before ganne ryde
To the Joyus Garde, that ryche towne,
And sette a sege on iche a syde.

Aboute the Joyus Garde they laye   2110
112V   Seventene wokys and well mare,
Tille it felle uppon a day
Launcelot home bad hem fare,

"Breke youre sege, wendys awaye,
You to slae grete pyte it ware." 2115
He sayd, "Allas and weil-awaye,
That evyr beganne thys sorewe sare."

Evir the kynge and Syr Gawayne
Calde hym fals recreante knyght,
And sayde he had hys bretherne slayne, 2120
And treytour was by day and nyght,
Bad hym come and prove hys mayne
In the felde with hem to fyghte.
Launcelot sighed, for sothe to sayne,
Grete duelle it was to se with sight. 2125

So loude they Launcelot gonne ascrye
With vois and hydous hornys bere;
Bors de Gawnes standis hym by,
And Launcelot makys yvelle chere.
"Syr," he sayd, "wharefore and why 2130
Shulde we these proude wordys here?
Me thynke ye fare as cowardlye,
As we ne durste no man nyghe nere.

Dight we us in ryche araye,
Bothe with spere and with shelde, 2135
As swithe as evyr that we maye,
And ryde we oute into the felde.
Whyle my lyffe laste maye,
Thys day I ne shall my wepen yelde.
Therefore, my lyffe I darre wele laye, 2140
We two shall make hem all to helde."

"Allas," quod Launcelot, "wo is me
That evyr shuld I se with syghte
Aʒeyne my lord for to be,
The noble kynge that made me knyght. 2145
Syr Gawayne, I beseche the,

As thou arte man of myche myght,
In the felde let not my lorde be
Ne that thyselfe with me not fyghte."

It may no lenger for to byde,   2150
But buskyd hem and made all bowne.
Whan thay were redy for to ryde,
They reysed spere and gonfanoune.
Whan these ostes gan samen glyde
Withe vois and hydous hornys sowne,   2155
Grete pyte was on eyther syde
So fele goode ther were layd downe.

Syr Lyonelle with myche mayne,
Withe a spere byfore gan founde,
Syr Gawayne rydys hym agayne.   2160
Hors and man he bare to grounde,
That all men wende he had ben slayne.
Syr Lyonelle hade suche a wounde,
Oute of the felde was he drayne,
For he was seke and sore unsounde.   2165

In all the felde that ilke tyde
Myght no man stonde Launcelot aȝeyne,
And sythen as faste as he myght ryde,
To save that no man sholde be slayne.
The kynge was evyr nere besyde   2170
And hewe on hym with all hys mayne;
And he so corteise was that tyde,
O dynte that he nolde smyte agayne.

Bors de Gawnes saughe at laste,
And to the kynge than gan he ryde,   2175
And on hys helme he hytte so faste
That nere he loste all hys pryde.
The stede rigge undyr hym braste,
That he to grounde felle that tyde.

113R

And sythen wordys loude he caste   2180
Withe Syr Launcelot to chyde,

"Syr, shalthou all day suffer so
That the kynge shall the assayle,
And sethe hys herte is so thro,
Thy corteise may not availe.   2185
Batailles shall there nevere be mo
And thou wilt do be my consalle:
Zevyth us leve them all to slo,
For thou haste venquesshid thys bataille."

"Allas," quod Launcelot, "wo is me   2190
That evyr shulde I se with syghte
Byfore me hym unhorsyd bee,
The noble kynge that made me knyght."
He was than so corteise and fre,
That downe of hys stede he lyghte;   2195
The kynge theron than horsys he,
And bade hym fle yiffe that he myght.

113V   Whan the kynge was horsyd there,
        Launcelot lokys he uppon,
        How corteise was in hym more   2200
        Then evyr was in any man.
        He thought on thyngis that had bene ore,
        The teres from hys yȝen ranne.
        He sayde, "Allas," with syghynge sore,
        "That evyr yit thys werre began."   2205

The parties arne withdrawen awaye,
Off knyghtis were they wexyn thynne.
On morow, on that other daye,
Scholde the bataylle efte begynne.
Thay dyght hem on a ryche araye,   2210
And partyd ther ostes bothe in twynne.
He that byganne thys wrechyd playe,
What wondyr thoughe he had grete synne.

Bors was breme as any bore,
And oute he rode to Syr Gawayne,   2215
For Lyonelle was woundyd sore,
Wenge hys brother he wolde full fayne.
Syr Gawayne gonne aȝeyne hym fare
As man that myche was of mayne,
Eyther throughe other body bare   2220
That welle nere were they bothe slayne.

Bothe to grounde they felle in fere,
Therefore were fele folke full woo.
The kynges party redy were
Away to take hem bothe two;   2225
Launcelot hymselfe come nere,
Bors rescous he them froo,
Oute of the felde men hym bere,
So were they woundyd bothe two.

Off thys bataille were to telle,   2230
A man that it wele undyrstode,
How knyghtis undyr sadels felle,
And sytten downe with sory mode.
Stedys that were bolde and snelle
Amonge hem waden in the blode;   2235
Bot by the tyme of evyn belle,
Launcelot party the better stode.

Off thys batayle was no more,
Bot thus departen they that daye;
Folke here frendys home ledde and bare   2240
That slayne in the feldys laye.
114R   Launcelot gonne to hys castelle fare,
The bataille venquesshyd. For sothe to saye,
There was duell and wepynge sare:
Amonge hem was no chyldys playe.   2245

Into all landys northe and southe

Off thys werre the word spronge;
And yit at Rome it was full couthe
In Ynglande was suche sorowe stronge.
Thereof the pope had grete routhe, 2250
A lettre he selid with hys hande,
Bot they accorded welle in trowthe
Enterdite he wolde the lande.

Then was a bischope at Rome,
Off Rowchester, withouten lese, 2255
Tylle Ynglande he, the message, come,
To Karllylle ther the kynge was.
The popis lettre oute he nome,
In the paleis byfore the desse,
And bade them do the popis dome 2260
And holde Yngland in reste and pes.

Redde was it byfore all bydene,
The lettre that the pope gonne make,
How he moste have aȝeyne the quene
And acorde withe Launcelot du Lake; 2265
Make a pes hem bytwene
For evyrmore, and trews make,
Or Ynglande entyrdyted shulde bene
And torne to sorow for ther sake.

The kynge aȝeyne it wolde noȝte bene, 2270
To do the popys comaundemente,
Blythely ayeyne to have the quene,
Wolde he noght that Ynglonde were shente.
Bot Gawayne was of herte so kene
That to hym wolde he nevyr assente 2275
To make acorde hem bytwene
While any lyffe were in hym lente.

Through the sente of all bydene,
Ganne the kynge a lettre make.

The bysschope in message yede bytwene   2280
To Syr Launcelot du Lake,
And askyd yiffe he wolde the quene
Cortessly to hym bytake,
Or Yngland enterdyt shuld bene,
And torne to sorow for ther sake.   2285

Launcelot answeryd with grete favoure,
As knyght that hardy was and kene,
"Syr, I have stande in many a stoure
Bothe for the kynge and for the quene,
Full colde had bene hys beste towre   2290
Yiff that I nadde myselfe bene.
He quytes it me with lytelle honoure,
That I have servyd hym all bydene."

The bysschope spake withoute fayle,
Thoughe he were nothynge afroughte,   2295
"Syr, thynke that ȝe have venquysshid many a
                   bataille
Throwgh grace that God hathe for you wrought.
Ye shalle do now by my counsayle,
Thynke on hym that you dere bought.
Wemen ar frele of hyr entayle.   2300
Syr, lettes not Ynglande go to noght."

"Syr bysshope, castelles for to holde
Wete you wele I have no nede,
I myght be kynge yif that I wolde
Off all Benwike, that ryche thede,   2305
Ryde into my landys bolde
Withe my knyghtes styffe on stede.
The quene, yif that I to them yolde,
Off her lyffe I have grette drede."

"Syr, be Mary that is mayden floure,   2310
And God that all shall rede and ryght,

She ne shall have no dyshonoure,
Thereto my trouthe I shall you plyght,
Bot boldely brought into hyr boure
To ladyes and to maydons bryght,   2315
And holden in welle more honoure
Than evyr she was by day or nyght."

"Now yif I grande suche a thynge
That I delyvere shall the quene,
Syr bysshope, say my lorde, the kynge,   2320
Syr Gawayne, and hem all bydene,
That thay shall make me a sekerynge,
A trews to holde us bytwene."

115R
Then was the bysshope woundyr blythe
That Launcelot gaffe hym thys answere.   2325
Tylle hys palfray he wente as swythe,
And tylle Karllylle gonne he fare.
Tythandys sone were done to lythe,
Whiche that Launcelotis wordis ware;
The kynge and courte was all full blythe.   2330
A trews they sette and sekeryd thare.

Through the assent of all bydene,
A syker trews there they wrought.
Though Gawayne were of herte kene,
There ayenste was he noȝte   2335
To hald a trews hem bytwene
While Launcelot the quene home broght,
Bot cordemente thar hym nevyr wene
Or eyther other herte have sought.

A syker trews gonne they make,   2340
And with ther seales they it bande,
Thereto they thre bisshopys gon take,
The wiseste that were in all the lande,
And sent to Launcelot du Lake.

At Joyus Gard they hym fande,   2345
The lettres there they hym bytake,
And thereto Launcelot held hys hande.

The bisshopis than went on her way,
To Karlyll there the kynge wasse;
Launcelot shall come that other day   2350
Withe the lady proude in pres.
He dight hym in a ryche araye
Wete ye wele, withouten les;
An hundreth knyghtis, for sothe to saye,
The beste of all hys oste he chese.   2355

Launcelot and the quene were cledde
In robes of a riche wede,
Off samyte white with sylver shredde,
Yvory sadyll and white stede,
Saumbues of the same threde,   2360
That wroght was in the heythen thede.
Launcelot hyr brydelle ledde,
In the romans as we rede.

The other knyghtis, everychone,
In samyte grene of heythen lande,   2365
And in there kyrtelles ryde allone;
115V   And iche knyght a grene garlande,
Sadillis sette with ryche stone,
Ichone a braunche of olyffe in hande.
All the felde aboute hem schone,   2370
The knyghtis rode full loude synghand.

To the castelle when they come,
In the paleise gonne they lyghte.
Launcelot the quene of hir palfray nome;
They seyde it was a semly syghte.   2375
The kynge than salowes he full sone,
As man that was of myche myghte;

Feyre wordys were there fone,
Bot wepynge stode there many a knyghte.

Launcelot spake as I you mene,   2380
To the kynge of mykelle myght,
"Syr, I have the broght thy quene,
And savyd hyr lyffe with the ryght,
As lady that is feyre and shene,
And trewe is, bothe day and nyght.   2385
Iffe any man sayes she is noght clene,
I profre me therefore to feyght."

The Kynge Arthur answerys thore
Wordys that were kene and throo,
"Launcelot, I ne wende nevyr more   2390
That thow wolde me have wroght thys woo
So dere as we samen were,
There undyr that thou was my foo.
Bot noght forthy me rewis sore
That evyr was werre bytwexte us two."   2395

Launcelot than answeryde he
Whan he had lystenyd longe,
"Syr, thy wo thow witeste me,
And welle thou woste it is with wronge;
I was nevyr fer frome the,   2400
When thow had any sorow stronge;
Bot lyers lystenes thow to lye
Off whome all thys word oute spronge."

Than byspake hym Syr Gawayne,
That was hardy knyght and free,   2405
"Launcelot, thou may it noght withsayne
That thow haste slayne my brethrene thre;
Forthy schall we prove oure mayne
In feld whether shall have the gree.
Or eyther of us shall other slayne,   2410
Blythe shall I nevyr be."

116R Launcelot answeryd with hert sore,
Thoughe he were nothynge afroughte,
"Gawayne," he said, "thoughe I were there,
Myself thy brethren slow I noght,   2415
Other knyghtis fele ther were
That sythen thys werre dere han bought."
Launcelot syghed wonder sore,
The terys of hys yen sowght.

Launcelot spake as I you mene   2420
To the kynge and Syr Gawayne,
"Syr, shall I nevyr of cordemente wene
That we myght frendys be aȝeyne?"
Gawayne spake with herte kene
As man that myche was of mayne,   2425
"Nay, cordement thar the nevyr wene
Tylle on of us have other slayne."

"Sythe it nevyr may betyde
That pees may be us bytwene,
May I into my landys ryde   2430
Saffely, with my knyghtis kene?
Than wille I here no lenger byde,
Bot take leve of yow all bydene;
Where I wende in worlde wyde,
Engelond wolle I nevyr sene."   2435

The Kynge Arthur answered thore,
The terys from hys yȝen ranne,
"By Jhesu Cryste," he there swore,
"That all thys worlde wroght and wan,
Into thy landys whan thou willt fare   2440
The shall lette no lyvand man."
He sayd, "Allas," withe syghynge sare,
"That evyr yit thys werre byganne.

Sythe that I shall wende awaye,

And in myn awne landys wone,   2445
May I saffly wone ther aye
That ye wythe werre not come me on."
Syr Gawayne than sayd, "Naye,
By Hym that made sonne and mone,
Dight the as welle as evyr thou may,   2450
For we shall after come full sone."

Launcelot hys leve hathe taken thare,
It was no lenger for to byde;
Hys palfray found he redy ȝare,
Made hym redy for to ryde.   2455
Oute of the castelle gonne they fare;
Gremly teres lette they glyde.
There was dwelle and wepynge sare;
At the partynge was lytelle pryde.

To the Joyus Gard, the ryche towne,   2460
Rode Launcelot the noble knyghte.
Busked hem and made a bowne,
As men that were of myche myght.
Withe spere in hand and gonfanowne,
Lette they nouther day ne nyght,   2465
To an haven hight Kerlyon;
Ryche galleys there they fande dyght.

Now ar thay shyppyd on the flode,
Launcelot and hys knyghtis hende;
Wederes had they feyre and goode   2470
Wher hyr wille was for to wende,
To an haven there it stode,
As men were leveste for to lende.
Off Benwike blythe was hyr mode,
Whan Jhesu Cryst hem thedir sende.   2475

Now ar thay aryved on the stronde,
Off hem was fele folke full blythe.

116V

Grete lordis of the lande
Aȝeyne hym they come as swythe
And fellyn hym to fote and hande;   2480
For her lord thay gonne hym kythe,
At hys domys for to stande
And at hys lawes for to lythe.

Bors made he kynge of Gawnes,
As it was bothe law and ryght;   2485
Lyonelle made kynge of Fraunce,
Be olde tyme Gawle hyghte;
All hys folke he ganne avance
And landys gaffe to iche a knyghte,
And storyd hys castellys for all chance,   2490
For mykyll he hopyd more to fyght.

Estor he crownys with hys hande,
So sayes the boke withouten lese,
Made hym kynge of hys fadyrlande,
And prynce of all the ryche prese,   2495
Bad nothynge hym shulde withstande
Bot hald hym kynge as worthy was.
For ther no more hymself wold fande
Tylle he wiste to leffe in pes.

117R   Arthure wolle he no lenger abyde,   2500
Nyght and day hys herte was sore.
Messengerys did he go and ryde
Throughe-oute Yngland for to fare
To erlys and barons on iche a syde.
Bad hem buske and make all ȝare   2505
On Launcelot landys for to ryde,
To brenne and sle and make all bare.

At hys knyghtis all bydene,
The kynge gan hys conselle take,
And bad hem ordeyne hem bytwene   2510

Who beste steward were for to make,
The reme for to save and ȝeme,
And beste were for Bretaynes sake.
Full mykelle they dred hem all bydene,
That alyens the land wold take.   2515

The knyghtis answeryd withoute lese,
And said for sothe that so them thought
That Syr Mordred the sekereste was,
Thoughe men the reme throwoute sought,
To save the reme in trews and pees.   2520
Was a boke byfore hym brought,
Syr Mordreit they to steward chese;
That many a bolde sythen abought.

It was no lenger for to byde,
Bot buskes hem and made all bowne.   2525
Whan they were redy for to ryde,
They reised spere and gonfanowne;
Forthe they went with mykelle pryde
Tylle an havyne hyght Kerlyonne,
And graythes be the lande syde   2530
Galeis grete of fele fasowne.

Now ar they shippid on the see,
And wendyn ovyr the water wyde.
Off Benwyke whan they myght se,
Withe grete route they gonne up ryde,   2535
Withstode hem neyther stone ne tre,
Bot brente and slow on iche a syde.
Launcelot is in hys beste cyte;
There he batelle wolle abyde.

Launcelot clepis hys knightis kene,   2540
His erlys and hys barons bolde,
Bad hem ordeyne hem bytwene
To wete her wylle what they wolde:

117V

To ryde aȝeyne hem all bydene,
Or ther worthe walles holde,   2545
For well they wiste withouten wene
For no fantyse Arthur nold folde.

Bors de Gawnes the noble knyght
Stornnely spekys in that stounde,
"Doughty men that ye be dyghte,   2550
Foundis your worship for to fownd,
Withe spere and shelde and armes bryght,
Aȝeyne your fomen for to fownd.
Kynge and duke, erle and knyght,
We shall hem bete and brynge to grounde."   2555

Lyonelle spekys in that tyde,
That was of warre wyse and bolde,
"Lordyngis, yit I rede we byde,
And oure worthy walles holde.
Let them pryke with all ther pryde,   2560
Tylle they have caught bothe hungre and colde,
Than shall we oute uppon them ryde
And shredde them downe as shepe in folde."

Syr Banndemagew that bolde kynge
To Launcelot spekys in that tyde,   2565
"Syr, cortessye and youre sufferynge
Has wakend us wo full wyde;
Awise yow welle uppon thys thynge:
Yiff that they over oure landys ryde,
All to noght they myght us brynge,   2570
Whyle we in holys here us hyde."

Galyhud that ay was goode
To Launcelot he spekys thare,
"Syr, here ar knyghtis of kynges blode
That longe wylle not droupe and dare;   2575
Gyffe me leve, for crosse on rode,

Withe my men to them to fare.
Thoughe they be wers than outlawes wode,
I shall them sle and make full bare."

Off Northe Gales were bretherne seven,   2580
Ferly mekelle of strenghe and pryde,
Not full fele that men coude nevyne
Better dorste in bataile byde.

118R   All they sayd with one steven,
"Lordyngis, how longe wolle ye chyde?   2585
Launcelot, for Goddys love in heven,
With Galehud forthe lette us ryde."

Than spake the lord that was so hende,
Hymself, Syr Launcelot de Lake,
"Lordyngis, a whyle I rede we lende,   2590
And oure worthy wallys wake.
A message wolle I to them sende,
A trews betwene us for to take,
My lord is so corteise and hende
That yit I hope a pees to make.   2595

Thoughe we myght the worshyppe wynne,
Off a thynge myn hert is sore;
Thys land is of folke full thynne,
Bataylles has it made full bare,
Wete ye welle it were grete synne   2600
Crysten folke to sle thus more.
Withe myldenesse we shall begynne,
And God shall wische us wele to fare."

And at thys assent all they ware,
And sette a wacche for to wake,   2605
Knyghtis breme as any bare
And derfe of drede as is the drake.
A damyselle thay dede be ȝare,
And hastely gon her lettres make;

A mayde sholde on the message fare,   2610
A trews bytwene them for to take.

The mayde was full shene to shewe,
Uppon her stede whan she was sette:
Hyr paraylle all of one hewe,
Off a grene welvette.   2615
In hyr hand a braunche newe,
Forwhy that no man sholde her lette;
Therby men messangerys knewe
In ostes whan that men them mette.

The kynge was lokyd in a felde   2620
By a ryver brode and dreghe.
Awhile she hovyd and byhelde
Pavylons were pyghte on hyghe;
She saughe there many comly telde,
Wythe pomelles bryghte as goldis beghe;   2625
On one hynge the kyngis shelde,
That pavylon she drew hyr nyghe.

The kynges baner oute was sette,
That pavylon she drewe her nere.
With a knyght full sone she mette   2630
Hyght Syr Lucan de Bottellere.
She hailsed hym, and he her grette,
The mayde with full mylde chere,
Hyr erande was not for to lette,
He wiste she was a messengere.   2635

Syr Lucan downe gan hyr take,
And in hys armes forthe gan lede.
Hendely to her he spake,
As knyght that wise was undyr wede,
"Thou comeste from Launcelot de Lake,   2640
The beste that evyr strode on stede.
Jhesu, for Hys modyris sake,
Yiffe the grace wele to spede."

118V

Feyre was pight uppon a playne
The paviloun in ryche aparayle;   2645
The kynge hymselfe and Syr Gawayne
Comely sytten in the halle.
The mayde knelyd the kynge agayne,
So lowe to grounde gan she falle;
Here lettres were not for to layne   2650
They were irade amonge hem all.

Hendly and feyre the mayden spake,
Full fayne of speche she wold be sped,
"Syr, God yow save from wo and wrake
And all your knyghtis in ryche wede,   2655
Yow gretis wele Syr Launcelot du Lake,
That with yow hathe bene evyr at nede.
A twelve monthe trewse he wolde take
To lyve uppon hys owne lede.

And sythen yiffe ye make an heste   2660
He wille it holde with hys honde
Bytwene you for to make pees,
Stabully ever for to stonde.
He wolle rape hym on a resse
Myldely to the holy londe,   2665
There to lyve withouten lese
Whyle he is man lyvande.

The kynge than clepid hys counsayle,
Hys douȝty knyghtis all bydene,
Fyrste he sayde withouten fayle,   2670
"Methynke it were beste to sene;
He were a fole withouten fayle,
So feyr forwardys for to fleme."
The kynge the messyngere thus did assayle,
"It were pite to sette warre us bytwene."   2675

"Sertis, nay," sayd Syr Gawayne,

119R

"He hathe wroght me wo inoughe,
So traytorly he hathe my bredren slayne.
All for your love, Sir, that is treuthe,
To Yngland will I not torne agayne   2680
Tylle he be hangid on a boughe.
Whyle me lastethe myght or mayne,
Thereto I shall fynd peple inoghe."

The kynge hymself, withowten lese,
And iche a lord is nought to layne,   2685
All they spake to have pese,
But, hymself, Syr Gawayne.
To batayle hathe he made hys hest,
Or ellys nevir to torne agayne.
They made hem redy to that rese,   2690
Therefore was fele folke unfayne.

The kynge is comyn into the halle,
And in hys royall see hym sette,
He made a knyght the mayden calle,
Syr Lucane de Botteler, withouten lette.   2695
"Say to Launcelot and hys knyghtis all,
Suche an heste I have hym hette
That we shall wend for no walle
Tyll we with myghtis onys have mette."

The mayde had hyr answere,   2700
Withe drery hert she gan hyr dyght.
Hyr feyr palfrey fande she yare,
And Syr Lucan ledde hyr thedyr ryght.
So throw a foreste gan she fare,
And hasted her with all hyr myght   2705
There Launcelot and hys knyghtis were,
In Benwyk the browgh with bemys bryght.

Now is she went within the walle,
The worthy damysselle fayre in wede.

119V   Hendely she cam into that halle,   2710
       A knyght hyr toke downe of hyre stede;
       Amonge the pryncis proude in palle,
       She toke hyr lettres for to rede.
       There was no counsayle for to calle,
       But redely buskis them to that dede.   2715

       As folkys that preste were to feight,
       Frome feld wold they nevyr fle.
       But by the morow that day was lyght,
       Aboute bysegyd was all there fee.
       Ychone theym rayed in all ryghtis;   2720
       Nouther party thought to flee.

       Erly as the day gan sprynge,
       The trompettis uppon the wallis went.
       There myght they se a wondyr thynge
       Off teldys riche and many a tente.   2725
       Syr Arthur than, the comely kynge,
       With hys folkis ther was lente
       To yeff assaute, withoute lesyng,
       With alblasters and bowes bente.

       Launcelot all forwondred was,   2730
       Off the folke byfore the walle,
       But he had rather knowen that rease.
       Oute had ronne hys knyghtis all;
       He sayd, "Pryncis bethe in pease,
       For folyse fele that myght byfalle;   2735
       Yiff thay will not ther sege sease,
       Full sore I hope forthynke hem shall."

       Than Gawayne that was good at every nede
       Graythid hym in hys gode armour,
       And styffly sterte uppon a stede   2740
       That syker was in ylke a stoure.
       Forthe he sprange as sparke on glede,

Byfore the yates agayne the toure,
He bad a knyght come kythe mayne
A cours of werre for hys honoure.　　　　　　2745

Bors de Gawnes buskys hym bowne
Upon a stede that shuld hym bere,
With helme, sheld, and hauberke browne,
And in hys hand a full good spere.
Owte he rode a grete randowne,　　　　　　2750
Gawayn kyd he coude of werre;
Hors and man bothe bare he downe
Suche a dynte he yaffe hym there.

120R

Syr Lyonelle was all redy than,
And for hys broder was wonder woo,　　　　　2755
Redely with hys stede oute ranne,
And wende Gawayne for to sloo.
Gawayn hym kepte as he wele can,
As he that ay was kene and thro,
Downe he bare bothe hors and man,　　　　　2760
And every day som servyd he soo.

And so more than halfe a yere,
As longe as they there layne,
Every day men myght se there
Men woundyd and som slayne.　　　　　　　2765
But how that ever in world it were,
Suche grace had Sir Gawayne
Ever he passyd hole and clere,
There myght no man stand hym agayne.

Than it byffelle uponne a tyde,　　　　　　2770
Syr Gawayne that was hende and free,
He made hym redy for to ryde.
Byfore the gatis of the cyte,
Launcelot of treson he becryed,
That he had slayne hys bretherne thre,　　　2775

That Launcelot myȝte no lenger abyde,
But he ever a cowarde scholde be.

The lord that grete was of honoure,
Hymselffe Sir Launcelot du Lake,
Above the gatis uppon the toure,   2780
Comely to the kynge he spake,
"My lord, God save youre honoure,
Me ys wo now for yowre sake,
Agaynste thy kynne to stonde in stoure,
But nedys I muste thys batayle take."   2785

Launcelot armyd hym full wele,
For sothe had full grete nede,
Helme, hawberke, and all of stele,
And stifely sterte uppon a stede.
Hys harneyse lacked he nevir a dele,   2790
To were wantyd hym no wede,
No wepyn with all to dele.
Forthe he sprange as sparke on glede.

Than was it warnyd faste on hye,
How in world that it shuld fare,   2795
That no man schold come hem nye
Tylle the tone dede or yolden ware.
Folke withdrew them than bye;
Upon the feld was brode and bare,
The knyghtis mette as men it sye   2800
How they sette there dyntis sare.

Than had Syr Gawayne suche a grace,
An holy man had boddyn that bone,
Whan he were in any place
There he shuld batayle done,   2805
Hys strength shulld wex in suche a space
From the undyrtyme tylle none.
And Launcelot forbare ay for that case,
Agayne twente strokys, he yaff not one.

120V

Launcelot saw ther was no socoure,   2810
Nedysse muste he hys venture abyde;
Many a dynt he gan wele indure
Tylle it drew nere the noontyde.
Than he straught in that stoure,
And yaffe Gawayne a wond wyde;   2815
The blode all coveryd hys coloure
And he felle downe upon hys syde.

Throw the helme into the hede
Was hardy Gawayne woundyd so,
That unneth was hym lyfe levyd.   2820
On fote myght he no ferther goo,
But wightly hys swerd abowte he wavyd,
For ever he was bothe kene and thro.
Launcelot than hym lyand levyd,
For all the world he nold hym slo.   2825

Launcelot than hym drew on dryhe,
Hys swerd was in hys hand drawen,
And Syr Gawayne cryed lowde on hye,
"Traytor and coward, come agayne;
Whan I am hole and goynge on hye,   2830
Than wylle I prove with myght and mayne.
And yit a thow woldyst nyghe me nye,
Thow shalt wele wete I am not slayn."

"Gawayne, while thow myghtis styfflye stonde,
Many a stroke today of the I stode,   2835
And I forbare the in every londe
For love and for the kyngis blode.
Whan thou arte hole in herte and hond,
I rede the torne and chaunge thy mode.
Whyle I am Launcelot and man levande,   2840
Gode sheld me frome werkys wode.

But have good day, my lord the kynge,

121R

And your doughty knyghtis alle,
Wendyth home a leve youre werryeng,
Ye wynne no worshyp at thys walle;   2845
And I wold my knyghtis oute brynge,
I wote full sore rewe it ye shalle.
My lord, therefore thynke on suche thynge,
How fele folke therefore myght falle."

Launcelot that was moche of mayne,   2850
Boldely to hys cyte wente;
Hys good knyȝtis thereof were fayne,
And hendely hym in armys hente.
The tother party tho toke Syr Gawayne,
They wessche hys woundys in hys tente,   2855
Or ever he coveryd myght or mayne,
Unnethe was hym the lyffe lente.

A fortenyght the sothe to saye,
Full passynge seke and unsonde,
There Syr Gawayne on lechynge laye,   2860
Or he were hole all of hys wounde.
Than it byfelle uppon a day,
He made hym redy for to wound;
Byfore the yat he toke the way,
And askyd batayle in that stownd.   2865

"Come forthe Launcelot and prove thy mayne.
Thou traytor that hast treson wroght,
My thre brethern thou haste slayne,
And falsly theym to grounde brought.
Whyle me lastethe myght or mayne,   2870
Thys qarell leve wyll I noght,
Ne pees shall ther nevir be sayne,
Or thy sydes be throw sought."

Than Launcelot thoght it nothyng gode,
And for these wordis he was full wo.   2875

Above the gatis than he yode
And to the kynge he sayd so,
"Syr, me rewys in my mode
That Gawayne is in hert so thro.
Who may me wyte, for corsse on rode,   2880
Thouʒth I hym in bataylle sloo."

121V   Launcelot buskyd and made hym bowne;
He will boldely the batayle abyde
With helme, shelde, and hauberke browne,
None better in all thys worlde wyde   2885
With spere in hand and gonfanowne,
Hys noble swerd by hys syde.
Oute he rode a grete randowne,
Whan he was redy for to ryde.

Gawayne grypes a full good spere,   2890
And in he glydes, glad and gay;
Launcelot kydde he coude of were,
And evyn to hym he takys the way.
So stoutely they gan togeder bere,
That marvayle it was, sothe to say;   2895
With dyntis sore ganne they dere,
And depe wondys daltyn thay.

Whan it was nyghed nere hand none,
Gawayne strenghe gan to increse;
So bitterly he hewyd hym uppon,   2900
That Launcelot all forwery was.
Than to hys swerd he grypes anone,
And sethe that Gawayne wyll not sese,
Suche a dynte he yaffe hym one
That many a ryche rewed that resse.   2905

Launcelot sterte forthe in that stownde
And sethe that Gawayne will no sease;
The helme that was ryche and rownde,

The noble swerde rove that rease.
He hyt hym apon the olde wounde, 2910
That over the sadyll downe he wente,
And grysely gronyd upon the ground;
And there was good Gawayne shent.

Yit Gawayne swounynge there as he lay,
Gryped to hym bothe swerde and sheld, 2915
"Lancelot," he sayd, "sothely to saye,
And by Hym that all thys world shall welde,
Whyle me lastethe lyffe todaye,
To the me shall I nevir yeld,
But do the werste that evyr thou may, 2920
I schall defend me in the felde."

122R   Launcelot than full styll stoode
As man that was moche of myght,
"Gawayne, me rewes in my mode
Men hald the so noble a knyght. 2925
Wenystow I were so wode
Agaynste a feble man to fyght?
I wyll not now, by crosse on rode,
Nor nevir yit dyd by day nor nyght.

But have good day, my lord the kynge, 2930
And all youre douȝty knyghtis bydene,
Wendyth home and leve your werrynge,
For here ye shall no worshyppe wynne.
Yif I wolde my knyghtis oute brynge,
I hope full sone it shuld be sene; 2935
But, good lord, thynke uppon a thynge,
The love that hathe be us bytwene."

After was it monthes two,
As frely folke it undyrstode,
Or ever Gawayne myght ryde or go 2940
Or had fote upon erthe to stonde,

The thryd tyme he was full thro
To do batayle with herte and hande.
But than was word comen hem to
That they muste home to Yngland.   2945

Suche mesage was hem brought,
There was no man that thought it goode;
The kynge hymselfe full sone it thought,
Full moche mornyd he in hys mode,
That suche treson in Ynglond shuld be wroght   2950
That he moste nedys over the flode.
They brake sege and homward sought,
And after they had moche angry mode.

That fals traytor, Syr Mordreid,
The kynges soster sone he was,   2955
And eke hys owne sonne, as I rede,
Therefore men hym for steward chase.
So falsely hathe he Yngland ledde,
Wete yow wele withouten lese,
Hys eme-is wyffe wolde he wedde,   2960
That many a man rewyd that rease.

Festys made he many and fele,
And grete yiftys he yafe also.
122V   They sayd with hym was joye and wele,
And in Arthurs tyme but sorow and woo,   2965
And thus gan ryght to wronge goo.
All the concelle is noght to hele,
Thus it was withouten moo,
To hold Mordred in londe with wele.

False lettres he made be wroght,   2970
And causyd messangers hem to brynge,
That Arthur was to grownde broght,
And chese they muste another kynge.
All thay sayd as hem thought,

Arthur lovyd noght but warynge 2975
And suche thynge as hymselfe soght,
Ryght so he toke hys endynge.

Mordred let crye a parlement;
The peple gan thedyr to come,
And holly throwe there assente 2980
They made Mordred kynge with crowne.
At Canturbery ferre in Kente,
A fourtenyght held the feste in towne,
And after that to Wynchester he wente;
A ryche brydale he lette make bowne. 2985

In somyr, whan it was fayr and bryght,
Hys faders wyfe than wold he wedde,
And hyr hold with mayne and myght,
And so hyr brynge as byrd to bedde.
Sche prayd hym of leve a fourtenyght, 2990
The lady was full hard bestad,
So to London sche hyr dyght
That she and hyr maydens myght be cledd.

The quene whyte as lyly floure,
With knyghtis fele of her kynne, 2995
She went to London to the towre,
And speryd the gates and dwellyd therin.
Mordred changed than hys coloure,
Thedyr he went and wold not blynne;
Thereto he made many a shoure, 3000
But the wallys myght he nevir wynne.

The Archebysshop of Canterbery thedyr yode,
And hys crosse byfore hym broght.
He sayd, "Syr, for Cryste on rode,
123R   What have ye now all in your thoght? 3005
Thy faders wyffe whether thou be wood
To wedd her now mayste thou noght;

Come Arthur evyr over the flood,
Thow mayste be bold it wyll be boght."

"A, nyse clerke," than Mordred sayd,   3010
"Trowiste thow to warne me of my wille?
Be Hym that for us suffred payne,
These wordys shalt thou lyke full ylle.
With wilde hors thou shalt be drayne,
And hangyd hye upon an hylle."   3015
The bischoppe to fle than was fayne,
And suffred hym hys folyes to fulfylle.

Than he hym cursyd with boke and belle
At Caunterbery, ferre in Kente.
Sone, whan Mordred herd therof telle,   3020
To seche the bisschoppe hathe he sent.
The bysshop durste no lenger dwelle,
But gold and sylver he hathe hent;
There was no lenger for to spelle,
But to a wyldernesse he is went.   3025

The worldys wele ther he wyll forsake,
Off joye kepeth he nevir more,
But a chapelle he lette make
Bytwene two hye holtys hore.
Therein weryd he the clothys blake   3030
In wode as he an ermyte ware.
Often gan he wepe and wake
For Yngland that had suche sorowis sare.

Mordred had than lyen full longe,
But the towre myght he nevir wynne   3035
With strength ne with stoure stronge,
Ne with none other kynnes gynne.
Hys fader dred he evyr amonge,
Therefore hys bale he nylle not blynne.
He went to warne hem all with wronge,   3040
The kyngdome that he was crownyd inne.

Forthe to Dover þan gan he ryde,
All the costys wele he kende;
To erlys and to barons on ylk a syde

Grete yiftis he yaffe and lettres send,   3045
And forsette the see on ylke a syde
With bold men and bowes bente.
Fro Yngland that is brode and wyde,
Hys owne fader he wold deffend.

Arthur that was mykelle of myght   3050
With hys folke come over the flode,
An hundreth galeyse that were welle dyght,
With barons bold and hye of blode.
He wende to have landyd as it was ryght
At Dower ther hym thoght full gode,   3055
And ther he fande many an hardy knyght
That styffe in stoure agaynste hym stode.

Arthur sone hathe take the land
That hym was leveste in to lende.
Hys fele fomen that he ther found,   3060
He wende byfore had bene hys frend;
The kynge was wrothe and weliney wode,
And with hys men he gan up wend.
So strong a stoure was upon that stronde
That many a man ther had hys end.   3065

Syr Gawayne armyd hym in that stounde.
Allas, to longe hys hede was bare,
He was seke and sore unsond,
Hys woundis grevyd hym full sare.
One hytte hym upon the olde wounde,   3070
With a tronchon of an ore;
There is good Gawayne gone to grounde,
That speche spake he nevyr more.

Bold men with bowes bente

Boldely up in botes yode, 3075
And ryche hauberkis they ryve and rente
That throwowte braste the rede blode;
Grounden gleyves throw hem wente.
Tho games thoght theym nothynge gode;
But by that strong stoure was stente, 3080
The stronge stremys ran all on blode.

Arthur was so moche of myght
Was ther none that hym withstode,
He hewyd uppon ther helmes bryght
That throw ther brestes ran the blode. 3085
By than that endyd was the fight,
The false were feld; som wer fledde
To Canterbery, all that myght,
To warne ther master, Syr Mordred.

124R

Mordred than made hym bowne, 3090
And boldely he wylle batayle abyde
With helme, scheld, and hauberke browne;
So all hys rowte gan forthe ryde.
They hem mette uppon Barendowne
Full erly in the morowe tyde; 3095
With gleyves grete and gonfanowne,
Grymly they gan togedyr ryde.

Arthur was of ryche araye,
And hornys blew lowde on hyght,
And Mordred comyth glad and gay, 3100
As traytor that was false in fyght.
Thay faught all that longe day
Tyll the nyght was nyghed nyghe;
Who had it sene wele myght saye
That suche a stoure nevir he syghe. 3105

Arthur than faught with hert good,
A nobler knyght was nevir noon.

Throw helmes into hede yt yoode
And steryd knyghtis bothe blode and bone.
Mordred for wrathe was nye wode,   3110
Callyd hys folke and sayd to hem one,
"Releve yow, for crosse on rode;
Alas thys day so sone is goone."

Fele men lyeth on bankys bare
With bryght brondys throwowte borne;   3115
Many a doughty man dede was thar,
And many a lord hys lyfe hathe lorne.
Mordred was full of sorowe and care,
At Canterbery was he upon the morne;
And Arthur all nyght he dwellyd thare,   3120
Hys frely folke lay hym byforne.

Erely on the morow tyde,
Arthur bad hys hornys blowe,
And callyd folke on every syde,
And many a dede beryed on a rowe   3125
In pittes that was depe and wyde.
On iche an hepe they layd hem lowe,
So all that over gone and ryde
Som by there markys men myght knowe.

Arthur went to hys dyner thane,   3130
Hys frely folke hym folowed faste,
But whan he fand Syr Gawayne
In a shyppe laye dede by a maste,
Or evyr he coveryd myght or mayne,
An hundreth tymes hys hert nyghe braste.   3135
Thay layd Syr Gawayne upon a bere,
And to the castell they hym bare.

And in a chapell amydde the quere
That bold baron they beryed thare.
Arthur than changyd all hys chere;   3140

What wondyr thoghe hys hert was sare:
Hys suster sone that was hym dere,
Off hym shold he here nevyr mare.

Syr Arthur he wolde no lenger abyde,
Than had he all maner of evyll reste,   3145
He sought aye forthe the southe syde,
And toward Walys went he weste.
At Salusbury he thought to byde
At that tyme he thought was beste,
And calle to hym by Whytesontyde   3150
Barons bold to batayle preste.

Unto hym came many a doughty knyght,
For wyde in worlde theyse wordys sprange
That Syr Arthur hade all the ryght,
And Mordred warred on hym with wronge.   3155
Hydowse it was to se with syght:
Arthuris oste was brode and longe,
And Mordred that was mykell of myght
With grete gyftes made hym stronge.

Sone after the feste of the Trynyte   3160
Was a batayle bytwene hem sette,
That a sterne batayle ther shuld be,
For no lede wold they it lette.
And Syr Arthur makethe game and glee
For myrth that they shuld be mette,   3165
And Syr Mordred can to the contre
With fele folke that ferre was fette.

125R

At nyght whan Arthur was brought in bedd,
He shuld have batayle uppon the morow,
In stronge swevenys he was bystedde   3170
That many a man that day shuld have sorow.
Hym thowht he satte in gold all gledde,
As he was comely kynge with crowne,

Upon a whele that full wyde spredd,
And all hys knyghtis to hym bowne.   3175

The whele was ferly ryche and rownd,
In world was nevyr none halfe so hye,
Thereon he satte rychely crownyd,
With many a besaunte, broche, and be.
He lokyd downe upon the grownd,   3180
A blake water ther undyr hym he see
With dragons fele there lay unbownde,
That no man durst hem nyghe nyee.

He was wondyr ferd to falle
Amonge the fendys ther that faught.   3185
The whele overtornyd ther withall,
And everyche by a lymme hym caught.
The kynge gan lowde crye and calle,
As marred man of wytte unsaught;
Hys chambyrlayns wakyd hym ther withall,   3190
And woodely oute of hys slepe he raught.

All nyght gan he wake and wepe
With drery hert and sorowfull stevyn,
And agaynste day he felle on slepe;
Aboute hym was sette tapers sevyn.   3195
Hym thought Syr Gawayne hym dyd kepe,
With mo folke þan men can nevyn,
By a ryver that was brode and depe,
All semyd angellys cam from hevyn.

The kynge was nevyr yit so fayne   3200
Hys soster sone whan that he sye,
"Welcome," he sayd, "Syr Gawayne,
And thou myght leve welle were me.
Now, leve frend, withouten layne,
What ar tho folke that folow the?"   3205
"Sertis, syr," he sayd agayne,
"They byde in blysse ther I motte be.

Lordys they were and ladyes hende,
Thys worldys lyffe that hanne forlorne.
Whyle I was man on lyffe to lende, 3210
Agaynste her fone I faught hem forne;
Now fynde I them my moste frende,
125V   They blysse the tyme that I was borne.
They asked leve with me to wende,
To mete with yow upon thys morne. 3215

A monthe day of trewse moste ye take,
And than to batayle be ye bayne;
Yow comethe to helpe Lancelot du Lake
With many a man mykell of mayne.
To morne the batayle ye moste forsake, 3220
Or ellys certis ye shall be slayne."
The kynge gan woffully wepe and wake,
And sayd, "Allas, thys rewffull rayne."

Hastely hys clothys on hym he dyde,
And to hys lordys gan he saye, 3225
"In stronge sweyneys I have bene stad,
That glad I may not for no gamys gaye.
We muste unto Syr Mordred sende
And founde to take another day,
Or trewly thys day I mon be shende; 3230
Thys know I in bed as I laye.

Goo thow, Syr Lucan de Boteler,
That wyse wordys haste in wolde,
And loke that thou take with the here
Bysshopys fele and barons bolde." 3235
Forthe went they all in fere,
In trew bokys as it is tolde,
To Syr Mordred and hys lordis there they were,
And an hundreth knyghtis all untolde.

The knyghtis that ware of grete valoure, 3240

Byfore Syr Mordred as they stode,
They gretyn hym with grete honowre,
As barons bold and hye of blode,
"Ryght wele the gretys Kynge Arthur,
And praythe the with mylde mode   3245
A monethe day to stynte thys stoure,
For Hys love that dyed on rode."

Mordred that was bothe kene and bolde
Made hym breme as any bore at bay,
And sware, "By Judas that Jhesus sold,   3250
Suche sawes ar not now to saye.
That he hathe hyght, he shall it hold:
The tone of us shall dye thys day;
And telle hym trewly that I tolde,
I schall hym marre yife that I may."   3255

"Syr," thay sayd withowten lese,
126R   "Thowȝ thou and he to batayle bowne,
Many a ryche shall rewe that reasse
By all by dalte upon thys downe.
Yit were it better for to sease   3260
And lette hym be kynge and bere the crowne,
And after hys dayes full dredelesse
Ye to welde all Yngland, towre and towne."

Mordred tho stode stylle a whyle,
And wrothely up hys eyne there wente,   3265
And sayd, "Wyste I it were hys wylle,
To yeve me Cornwale and Kente,
Lette us mete upon yonder hylle
And talke togedyr with gode entente
Suche forwardys to fullfylle;   3270
Thereto shall I me sone assent.

And yiffe we may with spechys spede,
With trew trowthes of entayle,

Hold the bodeworde that we bede
To yeve me Kente and Cornwayle,   3275
Trew love shall ther lenge and lende.
And sertis, forwardys yif we fayle,
Aythur to sterte uppon a stede
Styffely for to do batayle."

"Sur, wyll ye come in suche maner   3280
With twelve knyghtis or fourtene,
Or ellys all your strenghe in fere
With helmes bryght and hauberkys shene?"
"Sertys, nay," than sayd he thore,
"Othur warke thou thare not wene   3285
But bothe oure hoostis shall nyghe nere,
And we shalle talke them bytwene."

They toke ther leve withowten lese,
And wyghtely upon there way wente.
To Kynge Arthur the way they chese,   3290
There that he satte within hys tente.
"Syr, we have proferyd pease;
Yiffe ye wille therto assente,
Gyffe hym the crowne after your dayes,
And in yower lyffe, Cornwayle and Kente.   3295

To hys byheste yiffe ye will holde
And your trouthe trewly therto plyght,
Maketh all redy your men bolde
With helme, swerd, and hauberke bryght.
Ye schall mete uppon yone molde   3300
That ayther oste may se with syght;
126V
And yiff your foreward fayle to holde,
There is no bote but for to fyght."

But whan Arthur herd thys nevyn,
Trewly therto he hathe sworne,   3305
And arayed hym with batayles sevyn

With brode baners byfore hym borne.
They lemyd lyght as any levyn
Whan they shold mete upon the morne;
There lyves no man undyr hevyn   3310
A feyrer syght hath sene byforne.

But Mordred many men had mo,
So Mordred that was mykell of mayne
He had evyr twelve agaynste hym two
Off barons bold to batayle bayne.   3315
Arthur and Mordred bothe were thro
Shuld mete bothe upon a playne,
The wyse shuld come to and fro
To make acord, the sothe to sayne.

Arthur in hys herte hathe caste,   3320
And to hys lordis gan he saye,
"To yonder traytor have I no truste
But that he woll us falselly betraye.
Yiff we may not oure forwardys faste
And ye se any wepyn drayne,   3325
Presythe forthe as princes praste
That he and all hys hoste be slayne."

Mordred that was kene and thro
Hys frely folke he sayd toforne,
"I wote that Arthur is full woo   3330
That he hathe thus hys landys lorne.
With fourtene knyghtis and no mo
Shall we mete at yondyr thorne;
Yiff any treason bytwene us go
That brode baners forth be borne."   3335

Arthur with knyghtis fully fourtene
To that thorne on fote they fonde,
With helme, sheld, and hauberke shene,
Ryght so they trotted uppon þe grownde.

But as they acordyd shulde have bene,　　　　3340
An edder glode forth upon the grownde;
He stange a knyght that men myght sene
That he was seke and full unsownde.

Owte he brayed with a swerd bryght,
To kylle the adder had he thoghte.　　　　3345
Whan Arthur party saw that syght,
Frely they togedyr sought.

127R　　There was no thynge withstande theym myght;
The wend that treson had bene wroghte.
That day dyed many a doughty knyght,　　　3350
And many a bolde man was broght to noght.

Arthur stert upon hys stede,
He saw nothyng hym withstand myght;
Mordred owte of wytte nere yede
And wrothely into hys sadyll he lyght.　　　3355
Off acorde was nothyng to bede,
But fewtred sperys and togeder sprente;
Full many a doughty man of dede
Sone there was leyde upon the bente.

Mordred imaryd many a man,　　　　　　　3360
And boldely he gan hys batayle abyde:
So sternely oute hys stede ranne
Many a rowte he gan throw ryde.
Arthur of batayle nevyr blanne
To dele woundys wykke and wyde,　　　　　3365
Fro the morow that it byganne
Tylle it was nere the nyghtis tyde.

There was many a spere spente
And many a thro word they spake;
Many a bronde was bowyd and bente　　　　3370
And many a knyghtis helme they brake,
Ryche helmes they roffe and rente.

The ryche rowtes gan togedyr rayke,
An hundreth thousand upon the bente,
The boldest or evyn was made ryght meke.   3375

Sythe Bretayne owte of Troy was sought
And made in Bretayne hys owne wonne,
Suche wondrys nevyr ere was wroght,
Nevyr yit under the sonne.
By evyn levyd was there noght   3380
That evyr steryd with blode or bone,
But Arthur and two that he thedyr broghte,
And Mordred was levyd there alone.

The tone was Lucan de Botelere
That bled at many a balefull wound,   3385
And hys brodyr, Syr Bedwere,
Was sely seke and sore unsounde.
Than spake Arthur these wordys there,
"Shall we not brynge thys theffe to ground?"
A spere he gryped with fell chere,   3390
And felly they gan togedyr found.

He hytte Mordred amydde the breste,
And oute at the bakke bone hym bare.
There hathe Mordred hys lyffe loste,
127V   That speche spake he nevyr mare.   3395
But kenely up hys arme he caste
And yaff Arthur a wound sare
Into the hede, throw the helme and creste,
That thre tymes he swownyd thare.

Syr Lucan and Syr Bedwere,   3400
Bytwene theym two the kynge upheld;
So forthe went tho thre in fere,
And all were slayne that lay in feld.
The doughty kynge that was hem dere
For sore myght not hymself weld.   3405

To a chapelle they went in fere,
Off bote they saw no better beld.

All nyght thay in the chapelle laye
Be the see syde, as I yow newyn.
To Mary mercy cryand aye,   3410
With drery herte and sorowfull stevyn,
And to hyr leve Sonne gan they pray,
"Jhesu, for thy namys sevyn,
Wis hys sowle the ryght way
That he lese not the blysse of hevyn."   3415

As Syr Lucan de Boteler stode,
He sey folk uppon playnes hye.
Bold barons of bone and blode,
They refte theym besaunt, broche, and bee,
And to the kynge agayne thay yode   3420
Hym to warne with wordys slee.

To the kynge spake he full styll,
Rewffully as he myght than rowne,
"Syr, I have bene at yone hylle,
There fele folke drawen to the downe.   3425
I note whedyr they wyll us good or ylle;
I rede we buske and make us bowne,
Yiff it be your worthy wylle,
That we wende to som towne."

"Now, Syr Lucan, as thow radde,   3430
Lyfte me up whyle that I may laste."
Bothe hys armes on hym he sprad
With all hys strengh to hold hym faste.
The kynge was wondyd and forbled,
And swownyng on hym hys eyne he caste;   3435
Syr Lucan was hard bystadde,
He held the kynge to hys owne herte braste.

Whan the kynge had swounyd there,
By an auter up he stode;
Syr Lucan that was hym dere   3440
Lay dede and fomyd in the blode.
Hys bold brothyr Syr Bedwere
Full mykell mornyd in hys mode,
For sorow he myȝte not nyghe hym nere,
But evyr wepyd as he were wode.   3445

The kynge tornyd hym there he stode,
To Syr Bedwere with wordys kene,
"Have Excalaber my swerde good,
A better brond was nevyr sene,
Go caste it in the salt flode   3450
And thou shalt se wonder as I wene.
Hye the faste, for crosse on rode,
And telle me what thou haste ther sene."

The knyght was bothe hende and free,
To save that swerd he was full glad,   3455
And thought, "Whethyr I better bee
Yif nevyr man it after had;
And I it caste into the see
Off mold was nevyr man so mad."
The swerd he hyd undyr a tree,   3460
And sayd, "Syr, I ded as ye me bad."

"What saw thow there?" than sayd the kynge,
"Telle me now yif thow can."
"Sertes, syr," he sayd, "nothynge
But watres depe and wawes wanne."   3465
"A, now thou haste broke my byddynge.
Why haste thou do so, thow false man?
Another bode thou muste me brynge."
Thanne carefully the knyght forthe ranne,

And thought the swerd yit he wold hyde,   3470

And keste the scauberke in the flode.
"Yif any aventurs shall betyde,
Thereby shall I se tokenys goode."
Into the see he lette the scauberke glyde,
A whyle on the land hee there stode,   3475
Than to the kynge he wente that tyde,
And sayd, "Syr, it is done, by the rode."

"Saw thou any wondres more?"
"Sertys, syr, I saw nought."
"A, false traytor," he sayd thore,   3480
"Twyse thou haste me treson wroght.
That shall thow rew sely sore,
And be thou bold it shalbe bought."
The knyght than cryed, "Lord, thyn ore."
And to the swerd sone he sought.   3485

Syr Bedwere saw that bote was beste,
And to the good swerd he wente,
Into the see he hyt keste;
Than myght he se what that it mente.
There cam an hand withouten reste   3490
Oute of the water, and feyre it hente,
And brandysshyd as it shuld braste,
And sythe as gleme away it glente.

To the kynge agayne wente he thare,
And sayd, "Leve syr, I saw an hand,   3495
Oute of the water it cam all bare
And thryse brandysshyd that ryche brande."
"Helpe me sone that I ware there."
He lede hys lord unto that stronde;
A ryche shyppe with maste and ore,   3500
Full of ladyes there they fonde.

The ladyes that were feyre and free
Curteysly the kynge gan they fonge,

128V

And one that bryghtest was of blee
Wepyd sore and handys wrange.   3505
"Broder," she sayd, "wo ys me,
Fro lechyng hastow be to longe.
I wote that gretely grevyth me,
For thy paynes ar full stronge."

The knyght kest a rewfull rowne,   3510
There he stode sore and unsownde,
And sayde, "Lord, whedyr ar ye bowne?
Allas, whedyr wyll ye fro me fownde?"
The kynge spake with a sory sowne,
"I wylle wende a lytell stownde   3515
Into the vale of Aveloune,
Awhyle to hele me of my wounde."

Whan the shyppe from the land was broght,
Syr Bedwere saw of hem no more.
Throw the forest forthe he soughte   3520
On hyllys and holtys hore.
Of hys lyffe rought he ryght noght,
All nyght he went wepynge sore.
Agaynste the day he fownde ther wrought
A chapelle bytwene two holtes hore.   3525

To the chapell he toke the way,
There myght he se a woundyr syght.
Than saw he where an ermyte laye
Byfore a tombe that new was dyghte,
And coveryd it was with marboll graye,   3530
And with ryche lettres rayled aryght,
There on an herse sothely to saye
With an hundreth tappers lyghte.

Unto the ermyte wente he thare
And askyd who was beryed there.   3535
The ermyte answeryd swythe yare,

129R   "Thereof can I tell no more.
        Abowte mydnyght were ladyes here,
        In world ne wyste I what they were.
        Thys body they broght uppon a bere   3540
        And beryed it with woundys sore.

        Besauntis offred they here bryght,
        I hope an hundreth pound and more,
        And bad me pray bothe day and nyght
        For hym that is buryed in these moldys hore   3545
        Unto Ower Lady, bothe day and nyght,
        That she hys sowle helpe sholde."
        The knyght redde the lettres aryght,
        For sorow he fell unto the folde.

        "Ermyte," he sayd withoute lesynge,   3550
        "Here lyeth my lord that I have lorne,
        Bold Arthur, the beste kynge
        That evyr was in Bretayne borne.
        Yif me som of thy clothynge,
        For hym that bare the crowne of thorne,   3555
        And leve that I may with the lenge
        Whyle I may leve and pray hym forne."

        The holy ermyte wold not wounde;
        Sometyme archebishop he was
        That Mordred flemyd oute of londe,   3560
        And in the wode hys wonnyng chase.
        He thankyd Jhesu all of hys sound
        That Syr Bedwere was comyn in pease;
        He resayved hym with herte and honde
        Togedyr to dwelle withouten lese.   3565

        Whan Quene Gaynor, the kynges wyffe,
        Wyste that all was gone to wrake,
        Away she went with ladys fyve
        To Aumysbery, a nonne hyr for to make.

Therin she lyved an holy lyffe   3570
In prayers for to wepe and wake,
Nevyr after she cowde be blythe.
There weryd she clothys whyte and blake.

Whan thys tydyngis was to Launcelot broght,
What wondyr thowgh hys hert were sore.   3575
Hys men hys frendys to hym sought
And all the wyse that with hym were.
Her gallayes were all redy wroght;
They buskyd theyme and made yare,
To helpe Arthur was ther thoght   3580
And make Mordred of blysse full bare.

Lancelot had crownyd kyngis sevyn,
129V   Erlys fele and barons bold,
The nombyr of knyghtis I cannot nevyn,
The squyres to fele to be told;   3585
They lemyd lyght as any levyn.
The wynde was as hemself wold;
Throw the grace of God of hevyn,
At Dover they toke havyn and hold.

There herd telle Lancelot in that towne,   3590
In lond it is not for to layne,
How they had faught at Barendowne,
And how beryed was Syr Gawayne,
And how Mordred wold be kynge with crowne,
And how ayther of theym had other slayn,   3595
And all that were to batayle bowne
At Salysbery lay dede upon the playne.

Also in londe hert hyt kythe
That made hys hert wonder sare,
Quene Gaynor, the kyngis wyffe,   3600
Myche had levyd in sorow and care.
Away she went with ladyes fyve,

In lond they wyste not whedyr whar
Dolwyn dede or to be onlyve;
That made hys mornyng moche the mare.   3605

Lancelot clepid hys kyngis with crowne,
Syr Bors stode hym nere besyde,
He sayd, "Lordyngis, I wyll wend toforne,
And by these bankys ye shall abyde
Unto fyftene dayes at the morne.   3610
In lond whatsoevyr us betyde
To herkyn what lord hys lyffe hathe lorne,
Loke ye rappe yow not up to ryde."

There had he nouther roo ne reste,
But forthe he went with drery mode;   3615
And thre dayes he went evyn weste
As man that cowde nother yvell nor good.
Than syghe he where a towre by weste
Was byggyd by a burnys flode,
There he hopyd it were beste   3620
For to gete hym som lyves stode.

As he cam throw a cloyster clere,
Allmoste for wepynge he was mad;
He see a lady bryght of lere,
In nonnys clothyng was she clad.   3625
Thryse she swownyd swyftely there,
So stronge paynes she was in stad
That many a nonne than nyghed hyr nere
And to hyr chambyr was she ladde.

"Mercy, madame," they sayd all,   3630
130R   "For Jhesu that is kynge of blysse,
Is there any byrd in boure or halle
Hathe wrathed yow?" She sayd nay, I wysse.
Lancelot to hyr gan they calle,
The abbes and the other nonnys, I wysse,   3635

They that wonyd within the walle,
In counselle there than sayd she thus,

"Abbes, to you I knowlache here
That throw thys ylke man and me,
For we togedyr han loved us dere,   3640
All thys sorowfull werre hathe be.
My lord is slayne that had no pere,
And many a doughty knyght and free,
Therefore for sorowe I dyed nere
As sone as I evyr hym gan see.   3645

Whan I hym see, the sothe to say,
All my herte bygan to colde
That evyr I shuld abyde thys day
To se so many barons bolde
Shuld for us be slayne away.   3650
Oure wylle hathe be to sore bought sold,
But God that all myghtis maye
Now hathe me sette where I wyll hold.

Isette I am in suche a place;
My sowle hele I wyll abyde,   3655
Telle God send me som grace
Throw mercy of hys woundys wyde
That I may do so in thys place,
My synnys to amende thys ilke tyde,
After to have a syght of hys face   3660
At domysday on hys ryght syde.

Therefore, Syr Lancelot du Lake,
For my love now I the pray,
My company thow aye forsake,
And to thy kyngdome thow take thy way,   3665
And kepe thy reme from werre and wrake,
And take a wyffe with her to play,
And love wele than thy worldys make.
God yiff yow joye togedyr, I pray.

Unto God I pray, allmyghty kynge,   3670
He yeffe yow togedyr joye and blysse.
But I beseche the in all thynge,
That newyr in thy lyffe after thysse
Ne come to me for no sokerynge,
Nor send me sond but dwelle in blysse.   3675
I pray to God evyrlastynge
130V   To graunte me grace to mend my mysse."

"Now, swete madame, that wold I not doo.
To have all the world unto my mede,
So untrew fynd ye me nevyr mo;   3680
It for to do, Cryste me forbede.

Forbede it, God, that evyr I shold
Agaynste yow worche so grete unryght.
Syne we togedyr upon thys mold
Have led owre lyffe by day and nyght,   3685
Unto God I yiffe a heste to holde
The same desteny that yow is dyghte.
I will resseyve in som house bolde,
To plese hereafter God allmyght.

To please God all that I maye,   3690
I shall hereafter do myne entente,
And evyr foɪ yow specyally pray
While God wyll me lyffe lente."
"A, wylte thow so," the quene gan say,
"Fullfyll thys forward that thou has ment?"   3695
Lancelot sayd, "Yiff I sayd nay,
I were wele worthy to be brent.

Brent to bene, worthy I were,
Yiff I wold take non suche a lyffe,
To byde in penance as ye do here,   3700
And suffre for God sorow and stryffe.
As we in lykynge lyffed in fere,

By Mary moder, made, and wyffe,
Tyll God us departe with dethes dere,
To penance I yeld me here as blythe.   3705

All blyve to penance I wyll me take,
As I may fynde any ermyte
That wyll me resseyve for Goddys sake,
Me to clothe with whyte and blake."
The sorow that the tone to the tother gan make 3710
Myght none erthely man se hytte.
"Madame," than sayd Launcelot de Lake,
"Kysse me, and I shall wende as tyte."

"Nay," sayd the quene, "that wyll I not.
Launcelot, thynke on that no more;   3715
To absteyne us we muste have thought
For suche we have delyted in ore.
Lett us thynk on Hym that us hathe bought,
And we shall please God therfore;
Thynke on thys world how there is noght   3720
But warre and stryffe and batayle sore."

131R   What helpeth lenger for to spelle;
With that they gan departe in twene.
But none erthely man coude telle
The sorow that there bygan to bene.   3725
Wryngyng ther handis and lowde they yelle
As they nevyr more shuld blynne,
And sythe in swoune bothe downe they felle;
Who saw that sorow evyr myght it mene.

But ladyes than with mornyng chere,   3730
Into the chambyr the quene they bare,
And all full besy made theym there
To cover the quene of hyr care.
Many also that with Lancelot were,
They comforte hym with rewfull care.   3735

Whan he was coveryd, he toke hys gere
And went frome thense withouten mare.

Hys hert was hevy as any lede,
And lever he was hys lyffe have lorne;
He sayd, "Ryghtwosse God, what is my rede? 3740
Allas, forbare, why was I borne?"
Away he went as he had fled
To a foreste that was hym byforne;
Hys lyffe fayne he wold have levyd,
Hys ryche atyre he wold have of torne. 3745

All nyght gan he wepe and wrynge,
And went aboute as he were wode.
Erely as the day gan sprynge,
Tho syghe he where a chapell stode;
A belle herd he rewfully rynge. 3750
He hyed hym than and thedyr yode,
A preste was redy for to synge,
And Masse he herd with drery mode.

The arshebysshoppe was ermyte thare,
That flemyd was for hys werkys trew, 3755
The Masse he sange with syghyng sare,
And ofte he changyd hyde and hewe.
Syr Bedwere had sorow and care
And ofte mornyd for tho werkys newe;
Aftyr Masse was mornynge mare 3760
Whan iche of hem othyr knewe.

Whan the sorow was to the ende,
The byshope toke hys obbyte thare
131V　　　And welcomyd Launcelot as the hend,
And on hys knees downe gan he fare, 3765
"Syr, ye be welcome as oure frende
Unto thys byggyng in bankys bare,
Were it yower wyll with us to lende
Thys one nyght yif ye may no mare."

Whan they hym knew at the laste,   3770
Feyre in armys they gan hym folde,
And sythe he askyd frely faste
Off Arthur and of other bolde.
An hundreth tymes hys hert nere braste
Whyle Syr Bedwere the tale told.   3775
To Arthuris tombe he caste,
Hys carefull corage wexid all cold.

He threw hys armys to the walle
That ryche were and bryght of blee,
Byfore the ermyte he gan downe falle   3780
And comely knelyd upon hys knee.
Than he shrove hym of hys synnes alle,
And prayd he myght hys broder be
To serve God in boure and halle,
That myghtfull kynge of mercy free.   3785

That holy bisshope nold not blynne,
But blythe was to do hys boone.
He resseyvyd hym with wele and wynne
And thankyd Jhesu trew in trone,
And shroffe hym ther of hys synne,   3790
As clene as he had nevyr done none,
And sythe he kyste hym, cheke and chynne,
And an abbyte there dyd hym upon.

Hys grete hooste at Dover laye
And wende he shuld have comyn agayne.   3795
Tylle after byfelle upon a day
Syr Lyonell that was mekyll of mayne
With fyffty lordys, the sothe to saye,
To seche hys lord he was full fayne.
To London he toke the ryght way;   3800
Allas, for woo, there was he slayne.

Bors de Gawnes wold no lenger abyde,

But buskyd hym and made all bowne,
And bad all the oste homeward ryde,
God send theym wynd and wedyr rownd.   3805
To seke Lancelot wyll he ryde,
Ector and eche dywerse wayes yode,
And Bors sowght forthe the weste syde,
As he that cowde nowther yvell nor gode.

132R

Full erly in a morow tyde,   3810
In a foreste he fownd a welle;
He rode evyr forthe by the ryver syde
Tyll he had syght of a chapelle.
There at Masse thought he abyde,
Rewfully he herd a belle rynge,   3815
Ther Lancelot he fand with mekelle pryde,
And prayd he myght with hym there dwelle.

Or the halfe yere were comen to the ende,
There was comyn of there felowse sevyn,
Where ychone had sought there frend   3820
With sorowfull herte and drery stevyn.
Had nevyr none wyll away to wend
Whan they herd of Launcelot nevyn,
But all togedyr there gan they lend,
As it was Goddys wyll of hevyn.   3825

Holyche all tho sevyn yerys,
Lancelot was preste and Masse songe,
In penance and in dyverse prayers,
That lyffe hym thought nothyng longe.
Syr Bors and hys other ferys   3830
On bokys redde and bellys ronge,
So lytell they wexe of lyn and lerys,
Theym to know, it was stronge.

Hytte felle agayne an evyntyde,
That Launcelot sekenyd sely sare;   3835

The bysshop he clepyd to hys syde
And all hys felaws lesse and mare.
He sayd, "Bretherne, I may no lenger abyde,
My baleffull blode of lyffe is bare.
What bote is it to hele and hyde,   3840
My fowle flesshe will to erthe fare.

But Bretherne, I pray yow tonyght,
Tomorow whan ye fynde me dede,
Upon a bere that ye wyll me dyght
And to Joyes Garde than me lede;   3845
For the love of God allmyght,
Bery my body in that stede.
Sometyme my trowthe therto I plyght;
Allas, me forthynketh that I so dyd."

"Mercy, syr," they sayd all three,   3850
"For Hys love that dyed on rode,
Yif any yvell have grevyd the,
Hyt ys bot hevynesse of yower blode.
Tomorow ye shall better be,
Whan were ye but of comforte gode."   3855
Merely spake all men but he,
But streyght unto hys bed he yode,

And clepyd the bysshope hym untylle,
And shrove hym of hys synnes clene,
Off all hys synnes loude and stylle,   3860
And of hys synnes myche dyd he mene;
Ther he resseyved with good wylle
God, Maryis sonne, mayden clene.
Than Bors of wepyng had nevyr hys fylle,
To bedde they yede than all bydene.   3865

A lytell whyle byfore the day,
As the bysshop lay in hys bed,
A laughter toke hym there he laye

132V

That all they were ryght sore adred.
They wakenyd hym, for sothe to saye,   3870
And askyd yif he were hard bysted.
He sayd, "Allas and wele-away,
Why ne had I lenger thus be ledd.

Allas, why nyghed ye me nye
To awake me in word or stevyn.   3875
Here was Launcelot, bryght of blee,
With angellis thrytte thousand and sevyn;
Hym they bare upon hye,
Agaynste hym openyd the gatys of hevyn.
Suche a syght ryght now I see,   3880
Is none in erthe that myght it nevyn."

"Syr," thay sayd, "for crosse on rode,
Dothe suche wordys clene away.
Syr Lancelot eylythe nothynge but gode,
He shall be hole by pryme of day."   3885
Candell they lyght and to hym yode
And fownde hym dede, for sothe to saye,
Rede and fayer of flesshe and blode,
Ryght as he in slepynge laye.

"Allas, Syr Bors, that I was borne,   3890
That evyr I shuld see thys in dede,
The beste knyght hys lyffe hathe lorne
That evyr in stoure bystrode a stede."
Jhesu that crownyd was with thorne,
In hevyn hys soule foster and fede.   3895
Unto the fyfty day at the morne,
They lefte not for to synge and rede.

And after they made theym a bere,
133R   The bysshop and these other bold,
And forthe they wente all in fere   3900
To Joyes Garde, that ryche hold.

In a chapell amyddys the quere,
A grave they made as thay wold,
And thre dayes they wakyd hym there,
In the castell with carys cold.   3905

Ryght as they stode aboute the bere,
And to bereynge hym shold have browght,
In cam Syr Ector, hys brodyr dere,
That sevyn yere afore had hym sought.
He lokyd up into the quere,   3910
To here a Masse than had he thought.
For that they all ravysshyd were,
They knew hym and he hem nought.

Syr Bors bothe wepte and songe
Whan they that feyre faste unfold;   3915
There was none but hys handys wrange,
The bysshop nor none of the other bold.
Syr Ector than thought longe,
What thys corps was feyne wete he wolde;
An hundreth tymes hys herte nye sprange   3920
By that Bors had hym the tale tolde.

Full hendely Syr Bors to hym spakke,
And sayd, "Welcome, Syr Ector, I wysse,
Here lyethe my lord, Lancelot du Lake,
For whome that we have mornyd thus."   3925
Than in armys they gan hym take
The dede body to clyppe and kysse,
And prayed all nyght he myght hym wake,
For Jhesu love, kynge of blysse.

Syr Ector of hys wytte nere wente,   3930
Walowed and wronge as he were wode;
So wofully hys mone he mente,
Hys sorow myngyd all hys mode.
Whan the corps in armys he hente,

The terys owte of hys yen yode.   3935
At the laste, they myght no lenger stent,
But beryed hym with drery mode.

Sythen on there knees they knelyd downe,
Grete sorow it was to se with syght,
"Unto Jhesu Cryste aske I a boone,   3940
And to hys moder, Mary bryght;
Lord, as thow madyste bothe sonne and mone,
And God and man arte moste of myght,
Brynge thys sowle unto thy trone,
And evyr thow rewdyste on gentyll knyght."   3945

Syr Ector tent not to hys stede,
Whedyr he wold stynt or renne away,
But with theym to dwelle and lede,
For Lancelot all hys lyffe to pray.
On hym dyd he armytes wede,   3950
And to hyr chapell went hyr way.
A fourtenyght on fote they yede
Or they home come, for sothe to say.

Whan they came to Aumysbery,
Dede they faunde Gaynor the quene   3955
With roddys feyre and rede as chery;
And forthe they bare hyr theym bytwene,
And beryed hyr with Masse full merry
By Syr Arthur, as I yow mene.
Now hyght there chapell Glassynbery,   3960
An abbay full ryche of order clene.

Off Lancelot du Lake telle I no more,
But thus by leve these ermytes sevyn.
And yit is Arthur beryed thore
And Quene Gaynour, as I yow nevyn,   3965
With monkes that ar ryght of lore,
They rede and synge with mylde stevyn.

133V

Jhesu that suffred woundes sore
Graunt us all the blysse of hevyn, 3969

Amen.

Explycit le morte Arthur.

TEXTUAL NOTES

Following is a list of changes and corrections in the text either by the scribes or by the editor.

3 olde: MS old. This is one of a number of words to which J. Douglas Bruce added a final "e" to fill out the meter.

12 ende: MS end. See note 3.

106 Evwayne: MS Evwaye.

128 wight: MS might.

165 knight: MS knght. Also 1. 256.

284 swerde: MS swerd.

304 childis: MS chidis.

449 worlde: MS world. See note 3.

462 myght: MS mygh.

479 The second "a" in "imanased" is written above the line and is somewhat smaller than the other letters.

583 shewe: MS shew. See note 3.

626-627 These lines are between 11. 631 and 632 in the MS. The scribe indicates the change by putting a "b" in the margin opposite lines 628-629, and an "a" opposite these lines.

724 "lady" is written at the end of the line, and a caret indicates its place in the line.

754 dyskere: MS discovyr. Bruce emended this to make it fit the rhyme better.

775 hyrselfe: MS hyrself. See note 3.

832 Knyghtis: MS nyghtis. Normally the first letter of an indented stanza is written small on the margin side of the indentation, several spaces away from the rest of the line.

Presumably they are to be erased when a large capital is supplied. Here the scribe neglected to put this guide letter.

856 "b" is written smaller, above the line.

875 cloughe: MS swoughe. See 1. 893.

915 Thoughe þat: MS that thoughe þat.

919 "on" is written smaller, above the line. A caret indicates its place.

952 Now: MS ow. See note 832.

1000 The second "a" in Gawayne is written full size above the "y".

1042 open yt: MS openyd.

1059 "you" is written smaller, above the line.

1091 Last line written by first scribe.

1102 grete: MS gre.

1107 other with som: MS other whith som.

1136 mayden: MS myden.

1137 "hys" is written smaller, above the line.

1162 maners: MS meners.

1327 was in dede: MS was dede.

1328 were: MS werere.

1331 "wite" is written smaller, above the line.

1333 hertes: MS hetes.

1360 Mercy: MS Mecy.

1386 "me" is written at the end of the line; a caret indicates its place.

1413a Line inserted by F. J. Furnivall in his edition.

1426 The "a" in "mare" is written full size over a blotted letter in its place.

1441 "of" after "shulde" crossed out.

1487 "all dight" after "is" crossed out.

1490 though that: MS thought tha.

1544 ble: MS kne.

1545 "bors" after "that" crossed out.

1546 herte: MS hert. See note 3.

1551 knyght: MS knytht.

1554- "into the halle" after "Launcelot" in line 1554 crossed

1555 out. Obviously this belongs in line 1555, where the phrase is copied without the "to".

1561 "fyght" before "sythe" crossed out.

1574 wedis: MS wendis.

1577 "lyght" before "nyght" crossed out.

1578 that sythe: MS than sythe.

1645 "tyde" before "sythe" crossed out.

1653 "nolen" before "no lenger" crossed out.

1656 "all" written smaller, above the line.

1676 than sayde Syr: MS than sayde sayde Syr; "Gawayne" before "Agrawayne" crossed out.

1683 kynge: MS knyke.

1693 "such" after "of" crossed out.

1700 "thay" before "I" crossed out.

1706 "ned" written smaller, above the line.

1715 Than sayd: MS that sayd.

1726 now is made: MS now made.

1735 "to ney" after "wolde" crossed out.

1740 The "m" in "more" is blotted out. I take this to be accidental since all corrections in this are made by crossing out.

1756 "and" is written smaller, above the line. The twelve is written xij, one of many such instances in which the second scribe uses numerals. He uses xij in lines 1764, 1811, 2658, 3281, 3314; also, xx for twenty in line 2809; iij for third in line 2942; iij for three in lines 3399, 3402, 3616, and 3904; c for one hundred in lines 3052, 3135, 3239, 3374, 3533, 3543, 3774, and 3920; xiiij for fourteen in line 3336; ij for two in line 3382; xxx for thirty in line 3877; and vij for seven in line 3909. Based on forms used elsewhere in the work I have written these "thryd", "thre", "hundreth", "fourtene", "two", and "sevyn". I consulted the *OED* for "twelve," "twente," and "thrytte".

1763 The "a" in "abyde" is written smaller, above the line.

1802 "word wene" after "nevyr" crossed out.

1803 "wroght" before "dyght" crossed out.

1813 The first "e" in "treytoure" is written smaller, above the line.

1848 "sh" before "slayne" crossed out.

1925 forbrent: MS fo brent.

1936 "for" written smaller, above the line.

1952 "ryche of rente", with "many" written above it, before "many" all crossed out.

1991 "re" written smaller and above the line before "comfort".

1996 "fle" before "flore" crossed out.

2009 "was of" before "myche" crossed out.

2014 A blotted "a sq" at the beginning crossed out.

2028 "nevyr" before "nevyr" crossed out.

2029 "eyt" before "eyther" crossed out.

2030 "hym" after "gonne" crossed out.

2033 The "e" in "ladyes" is written smaller, above the line.

2036 "se" before "lende" crossed out.

2037 "styffe" with the beginning of an "r" at the end before "stiffe" crossed out.

2058 The "r" in "dwerffe" is written smaller, above the line.

2084 The "e" in "Gawnes" is written smaller, above the line.

2098 and: MS a.

2099 "sh" before "scottis" crossed out.

2117 "eveyr" before "evyr" crossed out.

2128 "standyr" before "standis" crossed out.

2132 "thynge" before "thynke" crossed out.

2153 "gounf" before "gonfanoune" crossed out.

2154- Folio 114R begins with these lines erroneously repeated.
2160 The only differences are that "layde" (1. 2157) is spelled "layd," and "rydes" (1. 2160) is spelled "rydys".

2174 "that" before "at" crossed out.

2204 "witht" before "with" crossed out.

2218 "hyr" before "hym" crossed out.

2230 A word is crossed out after "were".

2239 departen: MS depaten.

2246 Into: omitted in MS.

2257 "the" written smaller, above the line.

2284 Yngland enterdyt: MS Yngland end enterdyt.

2287 "fre" before "kene" crossed out.

2323 "dene" between "by" and "twene" crossed out.

2329 The "a" in "ware" written full size above a blot in its place.
2334 herte: MS hert. See note 3.
2343 "in all" after "wiseste" crossed out.
2345 Gard they: MS gard the they.
2350 "come" is written smaller, above the line.
2352 in: MS i.
2355 oste he chese: MS oste chese.
2366 "in" is written smaller, above the line.
2374 "hir" is written smaller, above the line.
2388 "spekys" before "answerys" crossed out.
2412 "fre" after "hert" crossed out.
2421 "of" after "kynge" crossed out.
2424 herte: MS hert. See note 3.
2434 worlde: MS world. See note 3.
2453 lenger: MS lenge.
2466 Kerlyon: MS kelyon.
2470 The second "o" in "goode" is written smaller, above the line.
2494 hys fadyrlande: MS fadyr lande hys. The "hys" is written
     smaller.
2498 ther no more: MS ther more.
2504 "Iche" before "iche" crossed out.
2529 "ane" before "an" crossed out.
2560 Let: MS le.
2562 "rydy" before "ryde" crossed out.
2585 The "n" in "Lordyngis" is written smaller, above the line.
2592 wolle: MS wlle. Bruce has a note pointing to spellings
     similar to that in Robert Mannyng, and the *OED* cites
     a few instances, but it seems to be a scribal error, really.
2602 An error in writing "myldenesse" is crossed out following
     "Withe".
2606 "Kyn" before "Knyghtis" crossed out.
2610 "of" after "sholde" crossed out.
2611 "make" before "take" crossed out.
2636 "downe" before "downe" crossed out.
2648 "kynge" before "mayde" crossed out.
2663 "for to sto" after "Stabully" crossed out; "fo" following
     that is crossed out, too.

2720 theym: MS theyne.

2725 many: MS may.

2739 "gode" is written smaller, above the line.

2741 "styff" before "syker" crossed out.

2795 shuld: MS shud.

2852 knyȝtis thereof: MS knyȝtis of.

2863 "hym" before "hym" crossed out.

2869 grounde: MS ground. See note 3.

2885 worlde: MS world. See note 3.

2902 "sw" or "fw" before "swerd" crossed out.

2909 swerde: MS swerd. See note 3.

2954 The "y" in "traytor" is written smaller, above the line.

2957 for: MS fo.

2968 "woo" before "moo" crossed out.

3026 "he" is written smaller, above the line.

3059 "wende" before "lende" crossed out.

3074 bente: MS bende with a "t" over the "n".

3094 "at" before "uppon" crossed out.

3113 The second "o" in "goone" is written smaller, above the line.

3170 swevenys: MS swevys.

3179 "richely" after "besaunte" crossed out.

3181 "he" after "ther" crossed out.

3182 "h" after "there" crossed out.

3187 "h" after "everyche" crossed out.

3193 sorowfull stevyn: MS sorowfull chere. The error may have
      existed in the scribe's source because he started to write
      "steven", crossed it out and wrote "chere", which does not
      fit the rhyme scheme.

3197 folke þan: MS folke tham þan.

3203 "leve" written smaller, above the line.

3250 Jhesus: MS Jhc, that is, Jesus Christ.

3261 lette hym be: MS lette be.

3265 "eyen" before "eyne" crossed out.

3279 "sst" before "styffely" crossed out.

3284 Sertys: MS Setys.

3289 "Whi" before "wyghtely" crossed out.

3304 "Arthr" before "Arthur" crossed out.

3327 "and" is an ampersand written smaller, above the line. It is not the ampersand the scribe normally uses.

3329 "fle" before "frely" crossed out.

3333 "and" before "at" crossed out.

3345 thoghte: MS thoghe.

3348 "that" after "nothynge" crossed out.

3374 An hundreth thousand: MS And C thousand.

3419 refte: MS Reste.

3448 swerde: MS swerd. See note 3.

3512 sayde: MS say.

3516 "w" before "vale" crossed out.

3536 "sone" after "swythe" crossed out.

3547 "bethe as" after "helpe" crossed out.

3554 "fo" before "som" crossed out.

3569 "hyr" is written smaller, above the line.

3586 as any levyn: MS as Any leme.

3628 many a nonne: MS many A man.

3637 sayd she thus: MS sayd they thus.

3672 beseche: MS beche.

3680 "more" before "mo" crossed out.

3681 "me" is written smaller, above the line.

3688 som: MS sam.

3711 "with syght" after "se" crossed out.

3735 with: MS w.

3752 "rodyd" before "redy" crossed out.

3760 mornynge: MS mornyge.

3765 "ganf" before "gan" crossed out.

3769 may no mare: MS may mare.

3774 nere: MS ne.

3780 ermyte: MS myte.

3806 "Ector" after "ryde" crossed out. The scribe apparently began line 3807 without going to the next line.

3821 "mode" after "drery" crossed out.

3855 A word is crossed out before "comforte".

3895 Line 3897 in MS; lines 3896 and 3897 are 3895 and 3896 respectively in the MS. The scribe indicates this change with a "b" and an "a" in the margin.

3920 The "e" in "nye" is written smaller, above the line.

3922 "ranne" before "spakke" crossed out.

3935 "went" before "yode" crossed out.

3940 The second "o" in "boone" is written smaller, above the line.

3965 "Gayon" before "Gaynour" crossed out.

EXPLANATORY NOTES

1 *Lordingis* This does not necessarily imply a noble audience, but is analogous to the generalized modern
term, "gentlemen". Chaucer's Pardoner uses it to address the pilgrims at the beginning of his *Prologue*.

5 *Arthur dayes* Uninflected genitives occur frequently
in this poem in proper names, titles, and other referrents
to persons: for example, *Th'erle sonne* (1. 426) and
soster sone (1. 3201). Regularly inflected forms also
occur: for example, *Arthurs knightis* (1. 260).

18ff. Bedroom scenes between Arthur and Guinevere are
rare: Bruce notes one in *De Ortu Waluuanii* (*PMLA*,
XIII, 424) and several such "bolster-conversations",
among them Laʒamon's *Brut*, 11. 3285 ff. Göller comments that Guinevere's concern for her husband's
reputation contradicts the spirit of the *Mort Artu*
(p.69).

35f. *shall ... worship wynne to dede of armys for to ryde*
There is a similar use of the infinitive as a gerund in
1. 2123.

54ff. There seems to be some confusion of traditions here.
He is both sick (1. 54), and making excuses to remain
for love of Guinevere (11. 55-56). When he finally goes
to see her, he says he just came to say good-bye (11.
75-78).

63 *with the dede* That is, in the act.

79 *Ya swithe that thou armyd be* Bruce, noting that a "verb
of wishing" is understood, attributes this construction

to the influence of the French *que* plus a subjunctive indicating a wish or command.

110 *is not to hyde* Bruce says, "This formula is more frequent in this romance than in any other". He cites its occurrence in a number of other romances.

117 *braundisshid yche a bone* The *OED* glosses this as "shake all over". Since it is this that enables Arthur to recognize Lancelot, we must assume that it means here a movement of the whole body with exceptional vigor. Bruce comments, "The verb is commoner used without direct object, and with sense of 'to swagger'". He does not offer any examples.

207f. Lancelot seems to assume the Maid will get over her infatuation.

309ff.   *Lancelot hytte on the hood*
      That his hors felle and he besyde.
      Launcelot blyndis in his blode.

That is, Lancelot hits Ector on the hood so that Ector's horse fell and he beside. Lancelot's vision is being impaired by his own blood. It is often helpful in reading this poem if one regards the line rather than the sentence as the sense unit.

343f. This is apparently Arthur's sentiment; presumably he feels that Lancelot would have a better chance of hearing of the tournament. He must not realize how severely Lancelot is wounded, since the purpose of the new tournament seems to be to bring him back.

389 *Forwhy þat* Bruce notes that its use as "provided that" is exceptional.

402 *a folyd knight* Bruce refers to *OED* fool (1) for "to fool" in an intransitive sense, and notes several other such uses.

460ff. *Th'erlys sonnys ... to serve them were nevir sadde, and th'erle hymselfe ... to make them bothe blyth and glad* The earl, too, was never "sad" to take care of his guests.

486f.   *Sir Lyonelle by God þan swore*
      That "myne wolle sene be evyrmore."

Bruce notes that direct discourse introduced by "that" is common in the Anglo-Saxon gospels and also appears in French, but is not common in Middle English.

595 *knew* As Bruce notes, it is subjunctive here.

603 *Launcelottis sheld de Lake* This construction with its lack of concord of appositives also occurs in 11. 644 f., *Th'erlis doughter ... off Ascolot.* This second example cannot be explained as an effort to make a rhyme.

632f. This is apparently the sentiment of both Arthur and Guinevere.

639 *semely* Substantive use of adjectives and adverbs is quite common in this poem.

697 *he wille with them ride* Apparently, Lancelot does not mean in their company; at any rate, they go home before him.

711 *The kinge hym kissyd and knight and swayne* The knights and swains kissed him, too.

717 No one was too tired to "dight" Lancelot as he would have himself.

758f. Guinevere seems to say that she will live in woe until she hears of Lancelot's death. Presumably she does not mean his death will make her happy, but that the source of her woe is that some other lady is enjoying his love.

764 *for crosse and rode* The more common form in this poem, *crosse on rode*, occurs in 11. 2576, 2928, 3112, 3452, 3882. Bruce suggests the latter is the original form, "cross" meaning the cross beam on Christ's cross. The *MED* has no such meaning, though the *OED* has *rood* in the sense of "rod" or "pole". The form, *corsse on rode*, (1. 2880) suggests a possible origin as "the (dead) body on the cross"; it is probably a transposition of letters, however.

841, 843 The repetition of *yif that he myght* is another indication that the sense unit is the line.

922ff. Arthur sets a day by which a knight must be found to fight for Guinevere with spear and shield, or else she will be executed.

991 *bayne* Seyferth takes this to mean "both". Bruce disagrees; he says it means "readily", and is derived from ON *beinn*. Bruce's reading is more likely, and the ON derivation supports Seyferth's opinions on dialect.

1481f. Lancelot seems to have forgotten what he was told of Guinevere's plight in 11. 932-949.

1537 *here hertys worde* Bruce interprets this as "the words they had spoken privily together". Rather, it is the silent communication between Bors and Lionel, based on what they secretly knew.

1557 *falle* Bruce notes this is past tense.

1630 Arthur takes Lancelot in his arms.

1662 *Hym* Sir Mador

1681 *oure eme sholde be* Arthur is their uncle. The *OED* has no really applicable definition for "should be".

1810 When Agravain and Sir Mordred came.

1814- No causal relationship is intended; they are two separate
1815 observations.

1825 *thes wordis* News of the affair. Lancelot was surely aware that it was common knowledge; he must mean that, by now, it has reached ears it should not have, as for example, Arthur's.

1829ff. The speaker is Lancelot.

1908f. The speaker is Arthur.

1942f. Lancelot sent the squire, not the tidings.

2024 *betwexte us* Between Gaheriet and Lancelot.

2066ff. This is the gist of the maiden's message; "hym" (1. 2066) refers to Lancelot; "they" (1. 2067) refers to Lancelot and Guinevere. This is not so much cynicism about trial by ordeal (when Lancelot defeated Mador, it was assumed that Guinevere was innocent, and the squires were tortured), as it is confidence that, with Lancelot, at any rate, might does make right. Arthur does, however, appear cynical (11. 2072-2073).

2095 All their care was directed toward preparation for the war, despite their losses and sorrows.

2180 *he* Bors de Gawnes.

2212 *He that byganne thys wrechyd playe* Agravain, apparently, not Lancelot.

2301 Göller points out that Arthur, in this poem, is an English king, and the downfall of Arthurian society is set here in England, rather than the geographically indefinite Logres (p. 68).

3008 The Archbishop of Canterbury does not appear to believe Mordred's story of Arthur's death. Mordred does not comment on his disbelief either.

3100 The impression that traitors who are false in fight are characteristically glad and gay is erroneous; these are two independent assertions.

3108 *yt* Excalibur, Arthur's sword.

3120 *thare* The battlefield at Barendowne.

3126ff. They bury the dead in a series of pits, but apparently identify some of the knights by markers, so that anyone going over the mounds would know some of those buried there.

3172 *gledde* Bruce accepts this as a variant of "cled" rather than emending it to "cled" as Seyferth suggested. He also reject Furnivall's gloss as "burning, glowing".

3260ff. Göller points to a similar arrangement in Hector Boece: "Arthuris ad vitae exitum in Britannia regnaret: eo vita functo Modredo ejusque inde liberis (si qui homini nascerentur) Britanniae regnum deferrentur." (p. 71)

3376f. Brutus, apparently, is being referred to.

3416ff. It is unclear whether Lucan is alone or not; in 1. 3420 it says "thay" went back to Arthur. Subsequent events suggest Lucan was more seriously wounded than Bedwer.

3419 "They" refers to the folk upon the plain; "theym", the slain barons.

3504ff. The lady is usually identified as Morgan le Fay.

3534ff. Although both Sir Mador (1. 898) and Sir Bedwer can read, the erstwhile Archbishop of Canterbury apparently cannot. While there is no particular need to insist on scrupulous accuracy in a romance, this is rather unbelievable.

3574 *thys tydyngis* The news of Mordred's treachery. Lancelot does not know what happened to Arthur since he left off besieging his city.

3815 *Rewfully* Modifies the bell's ringing; presumably the Archbishop and his fellows are still praying for the slain Arthur.

3887ff. Lancelot, like the Maid of Astolat and Guinevere, does not decay very quickly. Perhaps we are to believe that these great lovers, like some saints, have their corruption delayed.

GLOSSARY

With very few exceptions, nouns are given in the nominative singular and verbs in the first person present indicative forms; some inflectional variants are also listed, but very rarely noun plurals and verb forms in -s. Words with the i- or y- prefix are alphabetized under the second letter. No more than five or six line numbers are cited for words which occur more frequently.

a, adj.: all (2462).

a, conj.: and, if (2832, 2844).

abbyte, obbyte, n.: habit, attire of members of a religious or clerical order, the attire of a priest, hermit, etc. (3763, 3793).

abyde, v.: remain, stay (40); sojourn, dwell (327, 701); wait for (sb.) to do something (162, 628).

abye, v.: buy or pay for, pay the penalty for (1387, 2523); pret., *abought.*

acordement, n.: reconciliation, a covenant of peace (1639, 2028).

acountre, n.: attack, combat, encounter (1589).

acquyteste, v. 2 s. pres.: repay, reward (1550).

adrade, p. part.: afraid, frightened (1510, 1559).

adyght, p. part.: armed (1545).

afroughte, afryght, p. part.: afraid, frightened (1878, 2295, 2413).

after, adv.: about, concerning (1873).

agayne, prep.: in front of, in the presence of, before, in the sight of (2648); with verbs of motion: toward, to meet (709).

agilte, p. part.: sinned or transgressed against, offended, wronged (915, 1154, 1322); pret., *agulte.*

agoo, p. part.: gone, departed; of time: passed, elapsed (149).

agrevyd, p. part.: annoyed, incensed, resentful, angry (1169).

aʒeyne, adv.: see ayenste.

alblaster, n.: a crossbow, an arbalest, a weapon for discharging arrows, stones, etc., consisting of a bow set crosswise on a shaft (2729).

Allmyght, adj.: in the compound, *God Almight*, God Almighty (675, 3846).

also, adv.: as, also (1576).

alyen, n.: an alien, a foreigner (2515).

and, conj.: and, if (161, 239, 1706, 2846, 3945).

anone, adv.: at once, instantly, immediately, shortly (380, 1538).

antour, n.: see *aunter*.

appar(r)ayle, n.: furnishings, trappings (969); physical or moral equipment, personal characteristics (1748).

aparaylmente, n.: attire (2055).

are, *er*, adv.: before, earlier than the time when, until, up to the time that (291, 977, 1607, 2013).

arighte, adv.: truly, well (1034).

armyte, *ermyte*, n.: a religious recluse, a hermit (953, 3950).

arne, v.: see *bene*.

aryved, p. part.: reached land, came into port, disembarked, landed (2476).

as, conj.: as if (220).

ascrye, v.: to cry upon (an enemy), shout in defiance, challenge (2126).

assaute, n.: an armed attack or encounter, a siege (2728).

assay, v.: test, try (300).

assayle, v.: address (2674).

assent(e), n.: sentiment, attitude, opinion; *ben of assent*, be an associate or accomplice (1722, 1937, 2604).

aught, v., pret.: had, possessed, owned (653).

aunter(e), *auntre*, *auntur(e)*, *antour*, *aventure*, n.: an adventure, a venture, an enterprise, a knightly quest (33, 979); a tale of adventures, an account of marvelous things (19); fate, fortune, chance, one's lot or destiny (362, 1903).

auter, n.: the altar of a church (3439).

avance, v.: go forward, move forward (2488).

avauntement, n.: a boast; *maken avauntement*, to brag (1617).

aventure, n.: see *aunter*.

awayte, v.: be watchful, spy upon, keep under surveillance (64).

awise, v., refl.; bethink oneself, consider, take thought (2568).

ayeyne, adv.: once more, another time (2272).

ayenste, aʒeynste, aʒeyne, adv.: in opposition, hostilely against (1449, 1523, 1855, 1919, 1956).

aythur, ayther, outher, pron.: both of two, each of two (2013, 3278, 3301).

bale, n.: evil-doing, misdeed (3039); torment, pain, anguish, misery, grief, sorrow (628, 1074).

balefull, adj.: distressed, wretched, miserable (3839).

bande, v., pret.: obligated, bound, joined, fastened (2341).

bare, n.: boar, male swine. (229, 951, 2606).

bare, v.: bear, carry (1123, 1393).

batayle, n.: a body of warriors, esp. as ready for battle, an army or a division of it; troop, company, battalion (3306).

bayne, adj.: willing, inclined, eager (1134).

bayne, adv.: eagerly, quickly (991, 3217, 3315).

be, by, conj.: by the time that, when (1861, 1957, 3086).

becryed, p. part.: accused publicly (2774).

bede, v.: offer, make an offering, present (849, 1462, 3274); proclaim, announce, make known (32, 348).

bedene, bydene, adv.: with a n. or pron.: as a group, one and all, all together (70, 1513, 1684); *all bydene*: in all, all told (24, 1728).

be(e), n.: a piece of jewelry, a gem, a jewel, a treasure (3179, 3419).

beghe, n.: a ring (2625).

begredde, v., pret.: accused, charged (with a crime) (1812).

beld, n.: aid, support, help, encouragement, comfort (3407).

beleve, v.: depart from, leave (3963); leave, let remain or stay (558, 1765); remain, stay, tarry, dwell (60, 759); pret., *belefte, bylefte*.

beme, n.: a trumpet, esp., one used in warfare or hunting (2707).

bene, v.: be (1503); *bethe*, are, will be, be (1727, 1825, 1881); *arne*, are (2206); *by*, be (1759).

bente, n.: an open field, a battlefield (3359, 3374).

bente, p. part.: spread out or extended, stretched, fastened upon (990).

ibente, p. part.: set (with jewels), provided with stripes or borders, adorned or bordered (1035).

bere, n.: outcry, clamor, commotion, disturbance (2127).

bere, v., pret.: carried, bore, wore (538); refl., to conduct oneself (2747).

besaunt(e), n.: a gold Byzantine coin, any of several western European coins; a silver coin of western Europe; a bezant used as an ornament, an ornament resembling a bezant (3179, 3419, 3542).

besette, *bysette*, p. part.: bestowed, spent, employed, allocated (1412, 1568).

besy, adj.: busy (3732).

bethe, v.: see bene.

bette, v., pret.: flogged, beat, whipped, punished (13).

ble(e), n.: skin color, natural complexion (3504, 3779, 3876); countenance, face (739, 1544).

bloo, adj.: blue (151).

blynd, v.: become blind temporarily (311).

blynne, v.: cease (1691, 1824, 2999, 3364); come to an end, cease to exist (37); pret., *blanne*.

blyve, adv.: willingly, gladly, swiftly, promptly, immediately (3706).

bodden, p. part.: prayed; *bodden bone*: offered a prayer, obtained something prayed for (2803).

bode, n.: message, report, rumor (3468).

bodeworde, n.: a promise or pledge (3274).

boght, *bought*, p. part.: redeemed, saved, paid for, suffered for (470, 3009, 3483, 3718).

bold, adj.: confident, certain; *be thou bold*: you may be sure (3009, 3483).

bolde, adv.: confidently, with self assurance (3688).

bone, n.: bone, bone as one of the component parts of the body (117).

bo(o)ne, n.: a prayer, a favor asked for, a petition or request (1126, 2803, 3787, 3940).

bord, n.: a table (457, 859, 1369, 1504).

bote, n.: advantage, help, profit, good, benefit (3840); relief, deliverance, remedy, amends (3303, 3407, 3486).

bote, n.: a boat, a ship (964, 970, 975, 986, 3075).

bot(e), conj.: but, except, apart from, merely, only if, and yet (91, 199, 543, 649, 873).

bothis, num. gen.: both, each of two (176).

bounte, n.: knightly prowess, strength, valor, chivalry (125, 1739).

boure, n.: an inner room, esp. a bedroom (1809, 2314); *boure and hall*: chamber and hall (3632, 3784).

bowne, v.: get ready, gather troops (3175, 3596).

brandysshyd, braundisshid, v., pret.: flourished a weapon, vibrated, shook (3492, 3497); moved about energetically, proudly, or threateningly (117).

brast(e), v.: fall apart, break (2178); break because of pressure from within, burst (3077); of the heart: break or burst with emotion, pain, etc. (188, 1343, 1407).

braunchid, p. part.: having many branches, heavily wooded (891).

brayed, v., pret.: drew a sword, moved quickly or suddenly (3344).

breme, adj.: of persons: grim, fierce, cruel; of animals: ferocious, savage (229, 266, 951, 1600, 2101).

brenne, v.: burn, consume by fire (2507); suffer death or torture by fire (943, 1319, 1351, 1939); pret., *brente*; p. part., *brent(e)*.

brere, n.: a briar, a bramble, the dog rose (Rosa canina) (179, 724, 835).

brond(e), n.: a sword, a blade (3115, 3370, 3449).

browgh, n.: town, city, castle (2707).

ibrowghte, p. part.: to bring (sb.) into or out of a state or condition (1093).

browne, adj.: of steel, weapons, or armor: shining, polished, bright (284, 2748, 2884, 3092).

burne, n.: a watercourse of any size, spring, stream, river (3619).

busk(e), v.: make preparations, get ready, prepare (to do), prepare (sth.) (349, 1808); clothe, array, arm (2151); hurry, go hastily (547, 699); refl., prepare oneself (2151); *buskyd*, p. part.

by, v.: see *bene*.

bycalle, v.: charge, accuse (1553).

bydalte, p. part.: deprived or bereft, devoid, taken away (3259).

bydene, adv.: see *bedene*.

bydyng, n.: pleading, wishing, bidding (1134).

byggyd, p. part.: built, erected (3619).

byggyng, n.: a dwelling, abode, homestead, home, building, edifice (3767).

byheste, n.: promise, pledge, what is promised, request, commandment (3296).

byhold, v.: look at, gaze upon, pay attention to (97).

byknow, v.: acknowledge, admit, confess (916).

bylefte, v.: see *beleve*.

bymene, v.: signify or mean, symbolize, purport, betoken, portend (856).

byrd, n.: a young woman about to be married or just married, a bride (2989), a woman of noble birth, a lady (3632).

bysette, p. part.: see *besette*.

byspake, v., pret.: spoke out, objected to, condemned, contradicted, scolded (2404).

bytake, v.: hand over, deliver, surrender (2283, 2346).

care, n.: sorrow, sadness, grief (3905); gen., *carys*.

caste, v., pret.: take thought, consider, ponder (3320); move quickly, rush, dash (3776).

certes, sertis, sertes, sertys, adv.: certainly, surely, indeed (1180, 1395, 2676, 3284, 3479).

certeyne, adj.; adv.: certain; *in certeyne*: with certainty, for sure (928).

chase, v., pret.: see *chese*.

chere, n.: the face, facial expression, mein (477); manner, bearing, behavior (540, 781).

chese, v.: select or choose, elect, choose or take one's way (419, 514, 2355, 2957, 2973); pret., *chese, chase*.

claspid, v., pret.: made fast (a door) (1847).

cled, v., pret.: put clothing on, dressed (2993); clothed (in a particular way) (1836, 2356, 3172); p. part., *cledd(e), gledde*.

clepe, klepe, v.: call, summon, send for (106, 387, 536, 1444, 2540); 3 s., *klepis*; pret., *klepyd, klepitte*.

clongyn, p. part.: shrivelled up, wasted away, withered; *clongyn in clei*: waste away in the ground, molder as a corpse (751).

cloughe, n.: a narrow valley or dell, a ravine or gorge (875); gen., *cloughis* (893).

clyppe, v.: embrace (1801, 1547, 3927).

colde, v.: grow cold, be chilled; shocked, overcome (as with apprehension, grief, or remorse) (3647).

coloure, n.: skin color, complexion (2816).

comsement, n.: commencement, beginning (1726).

comynne, p. part.: come (1792).

consalle, conselle, n.: the act of discussing or conferring (956); counsel, advice, instruction (2187).

contre, n.: hostile meeting, onset, battle (3166).

corage, n.: the heart (as seat of the emotions), heart, spirit (3777).

cordement(e), n.: reconciliation, accord (2338, 2422, 2426).

corsse, n.: cross, the cross of Christ; a dead body, a corpse (2880).

corteise, n.: courtesy, gracious behavior, respect for others, kindness to others (2185, 2200).

corteise, co(u)rteyse, adj.: courteous, having manners of a courtly gentleman, gracious, respectful and kind to others (166, 623, 1050, 2172, 2194, 2594).

cortessly, adv.: courteously, politely, graciously (2283).

coste, n.: coast (3043).

coude, cowde, couth(e), v., pret.: have ability, capability, or skill (2751, 2892); know how, have a mastery of, be versed in (1675); know, be familiar with, possess knowledge (2248, 3617); p. part., *couthe*.

couth(e) v., pret.: could, was able (104, 223, 1446).

cover, v.: recover from illness or fainting, be restored, revive (3733, 3736); regain (one's health, strength) (2856, 3134); to heal (a wound) (2856, 3134); pret., *coveryd*.

craftely, adv.: skillfully (390).

crafty, adj.: clever, learned (877).

Cristene, Crysten, n., adj.: Christian (995, 2601).

crye, n.: a group of soldiers, company, troop, host, army (44).

crye, v.: proclaim, announce publicly (342).

dale, v.: give to, deliver (blows) (1076, 2897); pret., *daltyn*; p. part., *dalte*.

dare, v.: be dispirited, overcome, or stupified by emotion, be scared, tremble (with fear) (2575).

dede, n.: conduct, way of acting or of doing something (493, 1327); action, deed (916, 1747).

dede, n.: death, loss of life (911).

deffend, v.: forbid, deny; *deffend fro*: keep out of (3049).

dele, n.: a division, part, portion, a bit, a whit (2790).

dele, v.: have dealings; *dele with*: deal with, have to do with, cope with (2792).

departe, v.: take one's leave, depart; part company, separate (1805, 3704); divide, sever, split; portion out; of a marriage or love affair: be dissolved (743).

dere, n.: harm, injury, wound; grief (3704).

dere, adj.: excellent, noble, honored (1); valuable, precious (542); beloved, dear (756, 839, 3142).

dere, v.: hurt, injure, damage, wound, grieve (2896).

derelynge, n.: beloved person, sweetheart (1006).

derfe, adj.: bold, daring, audacious, forward (2607).

des(s)e, n.: a raised platform, dais, the place occupied by a king, a throne (1516, 2259).

devoyede, v., imper.: leave, go away, retreat from (1167).

deynge, n.: dying, death (1047).

dight(e), *dyght(e)*, v.: prepare, get ready for, deal with, do, perform (142, 167, 254, 326); refl., prepare oneself (1851); p. part., *dight(e)*, *dyght(e)*, *idighte*, arrayed, dressed, armed (1851).

do, *done*, v.: perform an action, do (1122); cause, make happen, cause to do (129, 2048); put, place (3224); *dostow*: do you (do) (69); pret., *did*, *dyd(e)*; imper., *dothe*; p. part., *done*.

doel(l)e, n.: see *duelle*.

dolwyn, p. part.: buried; *dolwyn ded*: dead and buried (3604).

dome, n.: order, command (2260); judgment, decision (2482).

dore, v.: stand, endure, tolerate (238).

dorste, v., pret.: see durste

doughty, *douȝty*, *duoghty*, adj.: bold, brave, valiant, strong in battle or combat, honorable, noble (24, 352, 789, 1051, 1076).

doughtynesse, n.: valor, prowess, might; fortitude (48).

doulfull, adj.: arousing or causing sorrow or distress, inflicting suffering or pain (1963).

duoghty, adj.: see *doughty*.

drake, n.: a dragon.

drayne, p. part.: drawn, dragged (859, 1850, 1997, 3014); carried (2164).

drechyd, p. part.: disturbed, troubled, frightened, distressed (1869, 1876).

dredelesse, adv.: securely, assuredly, certainly, surely (3262).

dreghe, adj.: great (2621).

droughe, v., pret.: pulled, tugged, drew (899, 1337, 1369); composed wrote (877).

droupe, v.: be afraid, cringe, cower; be downcast or sad, grieve, mourn (2575).

dryhe, n.: *drew on dryhe*: took aside (2826).

duelle, dwelle, doel(l)e, n.: the emotion of grief or sorrow (682, 1742); pain, suffering, torment (2125); the expression of grief or sorrow, lamenting, weeping, mourning (873, 2244).

dul(e)fully, adv.: sorrowfully, painfully, miserably (1406); *dulefully dight*: shamefully treated (2000).

durste, dorste, v., pret.: had the courage to, dared (727, 1799, 1874, 2133, 3022).

dwelle, v.: tarry, linger, remain, stay (1769, 1776, 1790, 1793).

dwellynge, ger.: tarrying, lingering, staying, remaining (80).

dwerffe, n.: dwarf (2058).

dyd(e), did, v., pret.: see *do*.

dyner, n.: dinner, a feast, usually the first big meal of the day, normally eaten between 9 a.m. and noon (3130).

dynt(e), n.: the blow of a weapon, stroke of a sword or lance (269, 470, 503, 1596); a wound made by a blow (484).

dyskere, v.: expose, disclose, make known, divulge, reveal (754, 1735).

dyverse, dywerse, adj.: different, divergent, separate (3807); numerous (3828).

edder, n.: a snake, a viper (3341).

efte, adv.: once more, again (2209).

ellis, adv.: else, as an alternative, as another possibility (943).

eme, n.: an uncle (1681, 2960); *eme-is*, gen.

endris, ender, adj.: *this endris dai*: recently, the other day (1017). Only occurs in such phrases.

entayle, n.: design, construction, ornamentation, decoration (975); the disposition of a person, the nature or essential character of a thing (2300, 3273).

entente, n.: *don entente*: take care, take pains, endeavor, pay attention, labor (3691).

enterdite, v.: place under the ban of the Church, cut off a nation from the public ministrations of the Church, place under an interdict (2253, 2268, 2284); p. part., *enterdyt, entyrdyted*.

er, adv.: see *are*.

ermyte, n.: see *armyte*.

everyche, pron.: every one, every single one (3187).

evyll, adj.: see yvelle.

evyn, n., evening (2236).

evyn, adv.: straight (3616).

eyle, v.: be troubled or afflicted; *eylythe nothynge but gode*: there is nothing wrong with (someone) (1992, 3884).

eyne, n. pl.: see *yen*.

falle, v.: belong, pertain, be appropriate, be fitting, suitable, needful (to or for a person, his nature or rank) (1119, 1122).

fande, v., pret.: came upon, met, discovered (2345, 2467, 2702, 3056); also used to state the existence, occurrence or location, without reference to a specific act of finding (2498).

fantyse, n.: deceit, guise (2547).

fare, n.: proceeding, doings, business (945).

fare, v.: travel, journey, come or go (156, 222, 249, 688).

fasowne, n.: physical makeup or composition, form, shape; style, fashion, manner (2531).

fast(e), adv.: eagerly, intently (1009, 1012).

faste, v.: make firm; establish securely, pledge, promise (3324).

fayne, feyne, adj.: joyful (604, 2852, 3200); willing, eager (1030, 3016).

fee, n.: livestock, moveable property, goods, riches (2719).

felau, felaw, n.: fellow, companion, comrade, colleague, a spiritual companion (1715, 3837).

feld, p. part.: slain, struck down, felled (3087).

fele, indef, num., as n.: many (2582); as adj.: many, much (6, 2019, 2032, 2157).

felle, adj.: fierce in combat, doughty, spirited, bold (228); treacherous, false, crafty, base, evil (1778).

felly, adv.: fiercely, violently (3391).

fellyn, v., 3 pl.: prostrates oneself, kneels before another person in reverence or supplication (2480).

felyd, v., pret.: felt, experienced a tactile sensation (485).

fende, n.: enemy, monster, demon (3185).

ferd, p. part.: afraid, fearful (3184).

fere, n.: a group of companions; *in fere*: in company, together; at the same time, all at once (2222, 3236, 3282, 3406, 3900).

fere, adj.: in health, well, strong; *hole and fere*: well and strong (411, 552).

ferly, adv.: wonderfully, exceedingly, extremely, very (6, 2581, 3176).

fer(re), adv.: to a distance, afar, far (134, 332, 439, 829, 2982).

fette, v.: go and get (3167); of death: take someone away (1067).

fewtred, v., pret.: couched or levelled (a spear), placed one's lance in a felt lined rest attached to the breastplate (*MED*) or saddle (Bruce) (3357).

feyght, n.: battle, fight, hostile engagement (1489).

feyght(e), v.: fight, contend with weapons, engage in armed conflict (1318, 1397, 1436).

feyr(e), adj.: pleasing to the sight, good to look on, beautiful (713, 962, 966, 994); of speech: eloquent, pleasant, agreeable, courteous (2673); comp., *feyrer*.

fleme, v.: reject an agreement (2673); expel, banish, exile, outlaw (3560, 3755); p. part., *flemyd*.

flode, n.: a flowing body of water, a river, stream (3619): the sea, any body of water (2951, 3051); water (as opposed to land) (966).

floure, n.: flower, prize; *mayden floure*: the best of maidens (2310).

folde, n.: the ground (3549).

folde, v.: bend, turn or twist (the head or body) (99); turn away, abandon, retreat (2547); embrace someone, receive joyfully or gladly (713, 3771).

fole, n.: a foolish, stupid, or ignorant person (2672).

folyd, p. part.: fooled, acted like a fool, silly (402).

folyse, n., pl.: stupidities, follies; harms, injuries, damages (2735).

fomyd, v., pret.: covered or flooded (with blood) (3441).

fone, n., pl.: enemies, those who hate or seek to injure someone (3211).

fone, num.: not many, few (2378).

fone, v.: grasp, seize, take hold of, pick up (1796).

fonge, v.: receive, welcome, take (into one's care) (3503).

for, prep.: in spite of, regardless of, notwithstanding (851).

forbare, v., pret.: spared (a person), refrained from killing (2836); endured (sorrow, affliction), bore with, tolerated, was patient, tolerant, lenient (3741); p. part., *forbare*.

forbede, v.: prohibit, forbid (3681, 3682).

forbled, p. part.: weakened or exhausted by loss of blood (3434).

forbrende, *forbrent*, p. part.: of a person: burned to death (1666, 1925).

for(e)ward, n.: agreement, contract, bargain (3302, 3324); terms of an agreement (2673, 3270).

forgid, p. part.: constructed, made, built (967).

forlorne, p. part.: lost completely and irrevocably, lost (a condition); *forlorne lyffe*: died, departed from life (3209).

forne, adv.: before, previously (3211).

forsette, v.: bar or obstruct by force, bar (passage by someone) (3046).

forthy, adv., conj.: for that, therefore, consequently, accordingly (1088, 2394, 2408); because (1141, 1878).

forthynke, v.: regret, repent, make sorry (2737, 3849).

forwery, adj.: exceedingly weary, exhausted (2901).

forwhy, conj.: in as much as, since, because (33, 97, 389); in order that, so that (2617).

forwondred, p. part.: amazed, astonished (2730).

foryelde, v., subj.: reward; *God foryelde the*: may God reward you (1548).

fote, n.: a linear measure of varying length, a foot (1593).

foule, n.: a bird, a domesticated fowl (1577).

founde, fownd(e), v.: proceed, go, set out (2551, 3337); depart, leave (1593, 2551); advance in attack, attack, thrust, strike (2159, 2553); pret., *fonde*.

fowle, adj.: evil, sinful, wicked; carrion (3841).

fre(e), adj.: noble in character, in appearance, gracious, generous, open handed (75, 90, 242, 408, 454).

frele, adj.: physically or morally weak, frail, unstable (2300).

frely, adj.: freeborn, noble, excellent (2939, 3121, 3131, 3329).

frely, adv.: nobly, generously, properly, rightly (3347, 3772).

freste, adv.: see *friste*.

freyned, v., pret.: inquired about, asked, inquired of (678).

friste, freste, adj., adv.: first (149, 736).

fro, prep.: from, away from (633); *ded fro*: removed by death (1979, 1987).

fyfty, adj.: fiftieth. An error for *fyfte*, "fifth"? (3896).

fykelle, adj.: changeable, variable, inconstant (1178).

gab, v.: lie, tell lies, report (sth.) untruthfully (1105, 1132, 1138, 1147, 1156); pret., *gabbyd*.

gaffe, v., pret.: see *yeff(e)*.

galeis, n., pl.: seagoing vessels having both sails and oars, galleys (2531).

galle, n.: poison (1654).

gam(e), n.: joy, happiness, gaity, festivity, revelry (96, 611); a pastime, amusement (3227); *maken game*: make sport, be entertaining (430).

gate, n.: way, manner; means, method; *thus gatys*: in this way (1712).

gayne, adv.: at once, directly, straight (1904).

gayne, v.: avail; *gayne to*: be useful to (sb. or sth.) (1071).

gere, n.: wearing apparel, clothes, dress; fighting equipment, armor, weapons, equipment of any kind, goods, possessions (3736).

geste, n.: a guest, a stranger or traveler entertained in one's home (453).

gilte, p. part.: sinned against, wronged (1377).

glad, v.: be gladdened, take pleasure, be comforted (3227).

gle, n.: entertainment, sport; mirth, rejoicing, amusement, merriment (96).

gledde, p. part.: see *cled*.

glede, n.: a live coal or brand, a spark (780, 2742, 2793).

gleme, n.: a beam or radiance of emitted light, a gleam; a type of what is evanescent or fleeting (3493).

glente, v., pret.: moved quickly; shone, flashed, glinted; *glente away*: glide away, vanish (3493).

glewe, n.: sporting jest, mockery; *maken glewe on*: make sport of (1164).

gleyve, n.: a lance, spear, a weapon with a long shaft ending in a point or an attached blade; a bill, gisarme; sword, falchion (3078, 3096).

glyde, v., pret.: slipped downward, descended, fell (2457); slithered, crawled (3341); pret., *glode*.

gon(ne), *gan(ne)*, v., pret.: came into existence, began, started, undertook, did (99, 139, 965, 1031, 1390); p. part., *gonne*.

goode, n.: good people; collectively, worthy men (2157).

go(u)nfanoune, *gonfanowne*, n.: a battle standard; the standard or banner of a king, an army, a division of an army, a troop (2104, 2153, 2464, 2527, 2886).

grande, v.: permit, allow, consent, assent, agree to (2318).

graythe, v.: prepare, make ready (2530); refl., prepare oneself, make oneself ready; dress, equip, arm (2739); pret., *graythid*.

grede, v.: cry out, shout, call out (791); weep, lament, mourn (1390); shout at, revile; *grede of treson*: to accuse of treason (1572).

gre(e), n.: victory in battle, tournament or combat; the prize for victory (48, 2409).

gremly, adv.: miserably, pitiably (2457).

grete, adj.: great, much (682).

gretlyche, adv.: injuriously, seriously, gravely, exceedingly (1152).

greve, v.: be physically painful (3069, 3852); refl: be sorry, lament (3508); injure, do harm (1781); pret., p. part., *grevyd*.

gronyd, v., pret.: groaned, moaned; was sick (2912).

grounden, p. part.: of weapons: sharpened, whetted (3078).

grysely, adv.: in a frightful manner, terribly, horribly; sorrowfully, pitiably (2912).

gyffen, v.: see *yeff(e)*.

gylte, n.: culpability, the state of being guilty, responsibility for a misdeed (1657).

gynne, n.: device, contrivance, a siege machine or tower; scheme, stratagem (3037).

ȝa, adv.: see *ya*.

ȝare, adv.: see *yare*.

ȝeme, v.: take care of, have charge of, guard, rule, govern (2512).

ȝender, adj.: see *endris*.

hailsed, v., pret.: greet, usually with respect, honor, or reverence; salute; address with reverence (2632).

hald, v.: hold, keep (89); keep from, deprive of (591); observe (2336); regard, consider (2497, 2925).

hale, n.: hall, main room (1078).

han(ne), *has*, v.: have (2417, 3209); have (sb. somewhere), keep (958).

harneise, n.: personal fighting equipment, body armor; as pl.: armor and weapons (1893).

haubarke, n.: a coat of mail, also plate armor or a coat of mail reinforced with plates (1515, 1541, 1831, 2106, 2748).

haven, havyne, n.: a harbor, port (2466, 2472, 2529).

hede, v.: look after, guard, protect (1417).

hedyr, adv.: to or toward this place, hither (134).

held(e), v.: bend, incline; yield, cease (261, 2141).

hele, n.: healing, cure, recovery; *sowle hele*: forgiveness of sin (3655).

hele, v.: conceal (sth.), hide, be silent, keep a secret (143, 466, 1473, 1678, 2967).

hem, pron.: them (1464, 2123).

hend(e), adj.: having the approved courtly qualities; noble, well-bred, refined; beautiful, handsome; valiant; gentle, mild (110, 166, 330, 541, 561).

hende, adv.: near, close (332).

hendely, adv.: in a courtly fashion, courteously, politely, graciously, generously (600, 1613, 2638, 2710, 3922).

hente, v., pret.: took hold of, siezed (1037); embraced (2853, 3934); caught (sb.) as he fell (3491); took (3023); p. part., *hent*.

herse, n.: a structure for carrying clothes, candles, statues, etc., placed over the coffin or erected over the tomb of a dead man (3532).

hest(e), n.: a promise, vow, agreement (2660, 2688, 2697, 3686).

hette, p. part.: see *hight(e)*.

heve, v.: raise, lift up (1998).

hight(e), *hyght(e)*, v.: give a person or place a specific name, call, have a certain proper name (93, 138, 883); promised, gave a promise, made a vow (1447, 3252); pret., p. part., hight(e), hyght(e); p. part., *hette*.

hit, it, yt, hytte, pron.: it (76, 3711, 3834).

hole, n.: hole; the lair of an animal; a hiding place or shelter (2571).

holly, holyche, adv.: completely, entirely, fully, wholly (935, 945, 2980).

holte, n.: a wood, grove, or copse (3029, 3521, 3525).

ho(o)ste, n.: an army (3286).

hope, v.: think, believe, suppose, expect, fear (490, 1491, 2491, 2737, 3620); pret., *hopyd*.

hore, adj.: gray, dark, gloomy (314, 3029, 3521, 3525, 3545).

horsyd, v., pret.: provided with a horse, mounted on a horse (87).

hovyd, hovid, v., pret.: waited around, hung about, remained, stayed, lingered (259, 2622).

hyde, n.: skin; *hyde and hewe*: in skin and complexion, in every way (3557).

hydous, hydowse, adj.: hideous to see, frightening, horrible (3156).

hye, hyghe, n.: haste, hurry; *on hye*: at once, quickly, very soon, fast (2623, 2794, 2828, 2830).

hynge, v., pret.: hung, fastened or mounted so that it hangs; hung on a hook, pin, etc. (2626).

hytte, pron.: see *hit*.

I-, occasional prefix with p. part, or pret.: see under second letter.

iche, yche, n.: each one (3761).

iche, yche, adj.: each and every, each, every (1685, 1732), *iche a*: each (117, 1561, 1646).

ichone, ychone. pron. phrase: each one, every one, every single one (419, 627, 2036, 2369, 2720).

ilke, ylk(e), adj.: same, identical (306, 1448, 1765, 1886, 2092).

ille, adv.: with hostility, aversion, displeasure, offence (1773).

inches(s)oun, n.: the reason or cause (1030); an excuse or pretext (56).

iwysse, adv.: certainly, assuredly, indeed, truly; often just a metrical tag (3633, 3635, 3923).

kende, v., pret.: had knowledge of, knew, was acquainted with (3043).

kene, adj.: brave, ardent, bold, valiant (795, 803); harsh (2071); forward, insolent (1820); of weapons: extremely sharp (1586).

kenely, adv.: fiercely, boldly; quickly (3396).

ken(n)e, v.: see, look at; recognize (175); be acquainted with, know (1097).

kepe, v.: have regard, care, reck (3027); pay attention or regard to (102); 3s. pres., *kepeth*; pret., *kepit*.

kest(e), v., pret., p. part.: uttered, placed, put, threw, cast (455, 3471, 3488, 3510).

kithe, v.: see *kythe.*

klepe, v.: see *clepe.*

klepitte, klepyd, v., pret.: see *clepe.*

knowlache, v.: confess, admit as true (3638).

kyd(de), v., pret.: see *kythe.*

kyd(de), p. part.: renowned, well-known, famous, notorious (2892).

kynne, n.: a class having common attributes; species, sort, kind (3037).

kyrtelle, n.: a man's tunic or coat, originally a garment reaching to the knees or lower, sometimes forming the only body garment, but more usually worn with a shirt below and a cloak or mantle above (2366).

kythe, kithe, v.: announce, proclaim, declare (1785); tell, show, prove, demonstrate (1441, 2751, 2892); exhibit, display, manifest (sth.) practically (2744); pret., *kyd(de)*.

lad(de), v., pret.: brought, took, conducted, guided (712, 723, 1506, 3629); p. part., *lad(d)e*.

lasse, adj., comp.: less, of not so great a degree, inferior (687).

layne, n.: concealment; *withouten layne*: without concealment or disguise (602, 1964, 3204).

layne, v.: conceal, hide; be silent about; *not to layne*: not to be concealed (989, 1026, 1108, 2650).

layne, v., pret.: lay, remained in that position, stayed (2763).

leche, n.: a physician (325, 331, 368, 380, 387).

lechyng, ger.: curing, healing, medical treatment (2860, 3507).

lede, n.: man, esp. one of the men or subjects of a king (3163); people, race, nation (653, 2659).

lede, v.: ?live (3948).

lees, *les(e)*, n.: untruth, falsehood, lying (276, 423, 992, 1719, 2255).

leff, *leve*, adj.: beloved, dear (1).

leffe, v.: live; pass life in a particular fashion (2499).

lefte, v., pret.: see *leve*.

lelyest, adv., superl.: most loyally, most faithfully, most truly (1066).

leme, n.: light, flame; a flash, ray, or gleam of light; brightness, gleam (see textual note for 3586).

lem(m)an, n.: a person beloved by one of the opposite sex, a lover or sweetheart (582, 586, 605, 637, 1013).

lemyd, v., pret.: shone, gleamed, lighted up (1471, 3308, 3586).

lende, v.: come to land; go ashore from a ship or boat, disembark (2473).

lend(e), v.: tarry, remain, stay, dwell, abide (565, 617, 988, 1007, 1353); pret., *lente*; p. part., *lente*.

lenge, v.: remain, abide, dwell (3556); continue to remain in a condition (3276).

lenger, adv.: longer (40, 162, 381, 565, 1484).

len(t)e, v.: lend, grant; grant temporary possession (1464, 3693).

lere, n.: the cheek; the countenance (also, its appearance) (3624).

lere, n.: see lore.

lere, v.: learn, acquire knowledge (641).

les(e), n.: see *lees*.

lesyng(e), n.: lying, falsehood (1004, 1043, 1098, 2728, 3550).

lete, v.: shed (1511); allow, permit (1530).

lette, v.: hinder, prevent (205, 2441); check or withhold oneself, desist (201, 665).

let(te), *lett*, v., pret.: caused, caused (to be made) (41, 2978, 2985, 3028).

levande, *lyvand*, part.: living, possessing life, being alive (949, 2840).

leve, n.: permission, leave (3556).

leve, adj.: dear, beloved (3204, 3412, 3495); preferable, willing, glad (2473, 3059); comp., *levir*; superl., *leveste*.

leve, v.: remain, continue to stay in a place (3203); depart from, quit, relinquish (2844); pret., *lefte*.

levyd, v., pret.: left, had remaining, were remaining (2820, 2824, 3380); departed from, quit (3744); pres. 2 s., *leviste*.

levyd, p. part.: lived, passed life in a certain way (3601).

levyn, n.: lightning, a flash of lightning; any bright flame (3586).

leyre, n.: the cheek, the face, countenance (475).

ligge, v.: lie, be recumbent (2824); lie in bed; *ligge by*: have sexual intercourse with (1730); part., *lyand*.

lofte, n.: *on lofte*: aloft, on top (846).

loggen, v., 3 pl. pres.: lodge, remain or dwell temporarily in a place (1901).

lokyd, p. part.: enclosed, surrounded; secured (2620).

lond, n.: land, country, nation (995, 1066).

lone, n.: concealment (1124).

lording, *lordyng*, n.: a form of address; in pl.: Sirs, Gentlemen (1, 226, 1952, 1960, 2018).

lore, *lere*, n.: learning, instruction (521); scholarship, teaching, religious doctrine (3966).

loreme, n.: the straps (often gilded or studded with metals or jewels) forming part of the harness or trappings of a horse (1471).

lorne, p. part.: lost, been parted from by chance or misadventure, been deprived of (3551).

loude, *lowde*, adj.: loud, strongly audible (910).

loude, lowde, adv.: openly, palpably; *lowde and stille*: under all circumstances (3860).

loughe, adj. from n. *lough*: a flame, blaze (1594).

loughe, v., pret.: laughed, expressed merriment or happiness by laughing (496, 1636); to smile at (1536).

lovyd, v., pret.: loved, felt attachment or affection (1021); ger., lovyng(e) (1092, 1102).

lyen, p. part.: dwell, sojourn (3034).

lyer, n.: liar, teller of falsehoods (2402).

lyght(e), n.: light, light as from a luminary, light as through a window (874).

lyght(e), adj.: bright, shining, luminous (2718, 3308).

lyght(e), v.: descend (from a horse), dismount (1562, 2063, 2195, 2373); fall into a condition, lodge in some position (581).

lykynge, ger.: pleasure, enjoyment; sensuality, lust (3702).

lymme, n.: a part or member of the body distinct from the head or trunk, a limb; any organ or part of the body (3187).

lyn, n.: contour, outline, lineament (3832).

lyre, n.: flesh, muscle, brawn (3832).

lythe, v.: hearken, listen (1772); listen to, hear (676, 1479, 1582, 1643).

lyvand, part.: see *levande.*

make, mache, n.: a mate, a spouse; a match, a person that is able to contend or compete with another as equal; a person that equals another in some quality (1062, 3668).

imanased, p. part.: threatened, menaced (479).

mare, adj., adv.: more, greater in degree (981); additional, further (1091, 1426); *lesse and mare*: altogether, as a whole (1125, 1606).

imaryd, v., pret.: harmed, injured, inflicted destructive bodily harm upon (3360).

may(e), n.: a maiden, virgin (195, 1107).

mayne, n.: physical strength, force, or power (269, 1658, 1960, 2004, 2009).

mede, n.: wages, recompense; reward, guerdon (3679).

mekell(e), mekyll(e), mykell(e), mykyll(e), mychelle, mochelle, adj., adv.: great in number, degree (269, 547, 735, 889); much, a great quantity (692).

mene, v.: complain, lament (727); lament for, mourn (3861).

mene, mynne, v.: say, tell, mention (22, 1686, 2380, 2420, 3695).

merely, adv.: pleasantly, cheerfully (3856).

mese, n.: serving of food, course of dishes (1512).

message, n.: a person conveying a communication, a messenger or envoy (2256).

mete, n.: a meal, a feast (442, 836, 939, 1486).

mete, v.: come or light upon, come across, fall in with, find (221, 1480, 2619, 2630); come together with, confer (3215, 3268, 3300, 3309, 3317); encounter or oppose in battle (303); come together in the shock of battle (1585); 3 s. and pl. pret., *mette*; 3 pl. pret., *metten*; ger. *metynge*.

meyne, n.: a body of retainers or followers; an army (2039).

mo, adv.: more, further, besides, in addition (190, 587, 648, 1699, 1895).

moche, myche, adj., adv.: great in size, stature, importance, number, quantity (1585); in great degree, greatly (1154); much (1918, 1960, 2009).

mochelle, adj.: see *mekelle*.

mode, n.: mind, heart, thought, feeling, frame of mind, disposition (386, 660, 1354, 1714, 1870).

modyr, n.: mother (2642).

mold(e), n. the ground, the earth (707, 1615, 3300, 3459, 3684).

mon, v.: may, shall (3230).

mone, n.: complaint, lamentation (765, 794, 814, 1085); lament (627).

monynge, ger.: complaint, lamentation (1384).

morrow, n.: morn, morning (3366, 3810).

moste, adj.: greatest (3212).

motte, v.: be permitted, be possible (3207).

mow(e), v.: may, be able, can (1114, 1140).

mychelle, mykelle, mykylle, adj., adv.: see *mekelle*.

myddis, n.: the middle, middle part or point, the midst (994).

myȝte, v., pret.: might, had ability or power, could (2776, 3444).

myngyd, v., pret.: disturbed, troubled, confounded (3933).

mynne, v.: see *mene*.

mysse, n.: wrong-doing, offence, misdeed (3677).

nade, ned, v., pret.: had not (1410, 1706).

nan, pron., adj.: none; *ore nan*: or not, or no (1149).

ne, adv.: not (76, 98, 566).

ned, v., pret.: see *nade*.

nede, n.: necessity, necessity arising from specific circumstances (59); difficulty, trouble (43, 85).

nedelyngis, adv.: necessarily, of necessity (753).

neghe, neyghe, nyghe, adv.: with verbs of motion: approach to; near (2832, 3183); nearly, almost, all but (1331, 1375, 1716).

nelle, v.: see *nylle*.

nere, v., pret., subj.: were not (411).

nevyn(e), newyn, v.: name, tell, make mention of (2582, 3304, 3409, 3584, 3823).

newe, adj.: new, recently brought into existence, different from what had been (1162).

no, adv.: not (37, 2907).

noblisse, n.: nobility, nobleness, the quality of being noble (1063).

noʒt(e), adv.: not, to no extent, in no way (1867, 1874, 1931, 1936, 2270).

nold(e), v., pret.: would not (128, 633, 701, 1109, 1126).

nome, v., pret.: took (2258, 2374).

none, adj.: no, not any (89).

noon, pron., adj.: not one, not any, no one, none (638, 3107).

note, v.: know not (3426).

nouther, pron.: neither (1593).

nye(e), v.: go, come or draw near to, approach closely (2832, 3183).

nyghe, adv.: see *neghe*.

nyghehande, adv.: almost, nearly (1591).

nylle, nelle, v.: will not (823, 1457, 1790, 2077, 3039).

nys, v.: is not, (there) is not (1455, 1531, 2011).

nyse, adj.: foolish, stupid (3010).

nyste, v., pret.: knew not (616, 856).

o, on, oon, num.: one (491, 586); a single (1593, 1602).

obbyte, n.: see *abbyte*.

of, adv.: off (213, 1850).

on, num.: see *o*.

one, adv.: alone (315).

onys, adv.: once, on one occasion (691, 2699).

oon, num.: see *o*.

ore, n.: grace, mercy, pity, clemency (1344, 3484).

or(e), adv., prep.: before, previously, formerly (526, 1740, 2202, 3375, 3717).

oryente, n.: the orient, Asia (2057).

oryson, n.: a prayer (1462, 1468).

oste, n.: an armed multitude, an army (2043, 2102, 2154, 2211, 2619).

overeste, adv.: in the highest or uppermost place (846).

outher, pron.: see *aythur*.

palle, n.: a fine or rich cloth, esp. as used for the robes of persons of high rank (2712).

paraylle, n.: clothing, array, attire, apparel (2614).

pas, n.: pace, rate of progression, speed in walking or running (1897).

payned, v., pret.: refl., took pains or trouble, exerted oneself, endeavored, strove (950).

pees, n.: freedom from or cessation of war or hostilities, peace (2012, 2429, 2520, 2662); a truce (2595).

pees, v., imper.: be silent, keep silence (1715).

pight, *pyghte*, p. part.: fixed and erected (as a tent or pavilion for lodgement) (2623, 2644).

play(e), n.: amusement, diversion, sport (398, 1019); enjoyment, joy, pleasure (779).

play(e), v.: amuse or divert oneself, sport, frolic (517, 730, 815, 890); exercise oneself (445).

playne, v.: make a complaint, complain (1143); 3 s. pres., *playnethe*.

pomelle, n.: a ball or spherical ornament; the ornamental top of a tent pole, flag staff, etc. (2625).

pre(e)s, *pres(s)e*, n.: a crowd, a throng, a multitude (280, 417, 518, 1713, 1955).

preson, v.: incarcerate, make a prisoner of, keep in a place of confinement (1853).

preste, n.: priest (3827).

preste, praste, adj.: ready in mind, inclined, eager, alert, keen (2716, 3151, 3326).

prevely, prewely, adv.: secretly (830, 1757); stealthily, craftily (1767).

previte, n.: one's private thought or counsel, private business (657).

profer, profre, v.: bring or put before a person for acceptance, offer (3292); make a proposal or offer; refl., offer or present oneself (2053, 2069, 2387).

pryde, pride, n.: magnificence, splendour, pomp, ostentation (141, 2560); elation of heart (52, 630, 1940).

pryke, v.: spur (a horse), ride fast, ride or advance on horseback (2560).

pryse, adj.: worthy, excellent, choice; a general term of appreciation (1111).

quere, n.: choir, the part of a church eastward of the nave in which the services are performed, the chancel (3138, 3902, 3910).

quest(e), n.: search or pursuit in order to find something (919, 925, 1320).

quite, adj.: free, clear (499).

quyte, v.: repay, reward, requite (2292).

radde, v., pret.: see *rede*.

irade, p. part.: read, scanned, perused (2651).

randowne, n.: impetuosity, great speed, force, violence (in riding, running, striking, etc.) (2750, 2888).

rap(p)e, v.: move with speed, hurry, rush (2664, 3613).

raught, v., pret.: started up (3191).

raunsowne, n.: release procured by paying a certain sum; the possibility of that release (943).

rayed, v., pret.: put (men) in order or array (2720): refl., made ready, prepared, equipped oneself (3306).

rayke, v.: go, move forward, esp. with speed (3373).

rayled, p. part.: adorned, set (with something) (3531).

rayne, n.: realm, kingdom (1980, 3223).

reas(s)e, res(s)e, n.: the act of rushing or running against others, an assault, attack, sally (1861, 1957, 2690, 2732); onward movement (2664).

reco(u)mforte, v.: to soothe, console, to strengthen or inspire with fresh courage (1493, 1499).

recreante, n.: cowardly, false, apostate (1833, 2119).

rede, n.: counsel or advice (907, 1113).

rede, n.: red, the color red (151, 3956).

rede, v.: rule, govern, guide (1416, 2311); direct, advise, counsel (168, 232, 3430); pret., *radde*.

redely, adv.: promptly, with alacrity or willingness, willingly, cheerfully (2715, 2756).

refte, v., pret.: committed spoliation or robbery, plundered (3419).

releve, v.: return or rally in battle (3112).

reme, n.: kingdom, realm (2512).

renne, v.: run; *renne away*: make off (3947).

rente, n.: revenue, income; income from land (2018).

rente, v., pret.: torn, lacerated (3076).

rescous, v., 3 s. pres.: rescues, saves, removes from danger (2227).

re(s)seyve, v.: receive, welcome (572); admit (sb.) into some relation with oneself (3708, 3788); take communion, accept God (3688, 3862).

rewe, v.: affect with regret, affect with sorrow, distress, grieve (1029, 1138, 2394, 2878); have, take, or feel pity or compassion; 3 s. pres., *rewith, reweth, rewis*; 3 s. pres. subj., *?rewdyste*.

rewf(f)ull, reufull, adj.: pitiable, lamentable, doleful, dismal (1085, 1980, 3223).

rewfully, adv.: in a doleful or dismal manner, sorrowfully (3815).

rigge, n.: the back or spine of an animal (2178).

right, adj., adv.: straight, direct, going straight toward its destination (161); straight, in a direct course or line (620).

rode, n.: a cross; Christ's cross (1350, 1392, 2576, 2928, 3851).

rode, n.: facial complexion (179, 3956).

roffe, rove, ryve, v., pret.: severed, divided (2909); pierced, rent, split (3076, 3372).

romans, n.: romance, a prose or verse tale of chivalry; the source, presumably the *Mort Artu* (2363).

roo, n.: rest, peace, repose (3614).

rought, v., pret.: took care, heeded, thought of, reckoned, considered (3522).

routhe, n.: the feeling of sorrow for another, compassion, pity (763, 2250).

rove, v., pret.: see *roffe*.

rownd, adj.: ?full, favorable (3805).

rowne, n.: a discourse, speech (3510).

rowne, v.: speak, talk, discourse (3423).

rowte, n.: a company, assemblage, band, or troop of persons (3093, 3363, 3373).

ryalle, adj.: having qualities befitting a king (1077).

ryche, n., adj.: one who is rich, powerful or noble (2905); powerful, noble, great (2108, 3373).

rydand, part.: riding, travelling or going on horseback (1555).

ryffe, adj.: rife, widespread; of words: commonly heard (1825).

ryghtwosse, adj.: just, guiltless, acting rightly or justly (3740).

ryve, v., pret.: see *roffe*.

sad(d)e, adj.: having had one's fill, satisfied, sated, weary or tired (of sth.) (461, 716).

salowe, *salue*, v.: salute (68, 735, 737, 2376).

samen, adv.: together, mutually (2154, 2392).

samyte, n.: a rich silk fabric worn in the Middle Ages, sometimes interwoven with gold (2056, 2358, 2365).

Sangrayle, n.: the Holy Grail (10).

sanzfayle, adv.: without fail, without doubt, doubtless (971).

sare, adv.: sorely; severely, dangerously, seriously (158, 272, 511, 802, 3033).

saugh(e), *sawgh*, v., pret.: see *sene*.

saumbu, n.: a saddle cloth (2360).

savely, adv.: without risk of error, in a safe manner (982).

sawe, n.: a saying, discourse, speech (1151, 3251).

sayne, v.: to say, utter or pronounce, to declare or state in words (2872, 3319); p. part., *sayne*.

scauberke, n.: the case or sheath for a sword (3471, 3474).

schroffe, v., pret.: see *shrove*.

scottis(s)he, *scottysshe*, *scottysche*, *shottysshe*, adj.: Scottish, of or belonging to Scotland or its people (839, 850, 878, 900, 938).

scryve, v.: of a wound: to open and discharge matter (383, 407).

se(a)se, v.: stop, discontinue, desist, leave off (996).

seche, v.: seek, go in search or quest of, try to find, look for (437, 3021, 3799); go to, resort to (870); go, move, proceed (2952); pret., p. part., *sought*.

see, n.: a seat; a seat of dignity or authority, a throne (2693).

se(e), *sey*, v., pret.: see *sene*.

seke, adj.: suffering from illness; ill, unwell, ailing (54, 158, 173, 525, 664).

seker, v.: to confirm by pledge or surety (2331).

sekereste, adj., superl.: most safe, most trustworthy (2518).

sekerynge, ger.: an assurance, a confirmation, pledge, securing (2322).

sely, adv.: wonderfully, marvelously (3387, 3482, 3835).

semblant, n.: the appearance or outward aspect of a person or thing (659).

semely, adj.: of a pleasing appearance, fair, well-formed; absol., a seemly person (639).

sene, v.: to see, perceive, distinguish, behold (706, 998, 2800, 3105, 3201); pret., *sawgh*, *saugh(e)*, *sye*, *sighe*, *syghe*, *se(e) sey*.

sengle, adv.: as a single thing, apart from others; uniquely (1795).

sente, n.: assent (2278).

sertis, *sertes*, *sertys*, adv.: see *certes*.

shende, n.: disgrace, ruin (1664).

shende, *shent(e)*, p. part.: destroyed, brought to destruction, discomfited (in battle) (1321, 1724, 2273, 2913, 3230).

shene, adj.: bright, shining, resplendent; beautiful (51, 68, 736, 1515, 1657).

shever, v.: tremble, shake, quiver (1408).

sho, pron.: she (1422, 1426).

shore, p. part.: ?removed by being cut (84).

shottysshe, adj.: see *scottis(s)he*.

shoure, n.: menace, threatening (3000).

shredde, n.: a length or end of gold or silver thread or lace (2358).

shredde, v.: to cut or hack in pieces, to cut down (2563).

shrove, schroffe, v., pret.: heard the confession of (sb.), administered absolution to (sb.) (3790).

shynand, part.: shining, being radiant, shedding beams of light; bright, gleaming (973).

sighe, v.: see *sene*.

sithen, sythen, sithe, sythe, adv.: afterwards, then (398, 614, 1530, 1700, 2660).

sithe, sethe, conj.: since (126, 209, 234, 557, 2903).

sitte, n.: care or sorrow; grief, trouble of any kind (497, 870).

slae, slo(o), v.: smite, strike, beat, to kill with a weapon, or generally by violence (843, 2115, 2507, 2579, 2601).

slee, adj.: knowing, wise, marked by secrecy (3421).

slyghly, adv.: wisely, quietly (1168).

snelle, adj., adv.: quick in movement or action, prompt, active (884, 2234); quickly, vigorously (790).

sokerynge, ger.: succouring, assistance, relief (3674).

sone, adv.: soon, within a short time, before long (930, 963, 1120, 1121, 2376).

soster, suster, n.: sister, female sibling; *suster sone*: nephew (2955, 3142).

soth(e), n.: truth, verity (60, 93, 226, 396, 771).

sothely, adv.: in or with truth, verily, truly (2916, 3675).

sought, v., pret.: see *seche*.

so(u)nd, n.: news, tidings (3562, 3675).

spede, v.: succeed, prosper; attain one's purpose or desire (1115, 1464, 2653); p. part., *sped*.

spelle, v.: talk, converse, speak (3024, 3722).

speryd, v., pret.: shut or closed firmly or securely (2997).

spill(e), v.: empty, disperse (23).

sprede, v.: draw or stretch out, as in torture (1392).

sprent(e), v., pret.: sprang, sprang forward, jumped, moved quickly or with agility (1846, 1892, 1949, 1954, 1994).

stable, adj.: steadfast in purpose or resolution, not fickle, changeable, or frivolous (1051).

stabully, adv.: in a stable manner, firmly (2663).

stad, p. part.: placed, put into a certain condition or plight (3226, 3627).

stede, n.: a person's office or position, his social position (851).

stent(e), v.: see *stynt(e)*.

stert(e), v.: leap or jump (2006); leap or spring (upon a horse) (2740, 2789, 3352); move with a bound or sudden violent impulse from a position of rest (857); pret., *stert(e)*.

steryd, v., pret.: moved, moved as a living human being (3381); roused to action, stimulated (3109).

steven, stevyn, n.: voice (3193, 3411, 3821, 3875); *with one steven*: with one voice, in accord (2584).

stiff(e), styff(e), adj.: stout, stalwart, sturdy (45, 228, 236, 263, 279).

stifely, styff(e)ly(e), adv.: stoutly, stalwartly, sturdily (2789, 2834, 3279).

stille, stylle, adj., adv.: motionless (760); without noise or commotion, quietly, silently (185, 359); secretly (206, 3860).

stode, n.: service, support (3621).

stomelyd, v., pret.: missed one's footing, tripped over an obstacle, stumbled (115).

stound(e), stownd(e), n.: a time, while, a short while, a moment (114, 1959, 2549, 2865, 3515).

stoure, stowre, n.: an armed combat or conflict, a contest in battle, a fight (236, 655, 1811, 2288, 2741).

stournely, stornnely, adv.: in a stern manner, severely, unbendingly, loudly (2549).

straught, v., pret.: stretched or extended, reached out (2814).

strode, v., pret.: straddled, bestrode (2641).

stronde, n.: strand, the shore of a body of water (2476, 3064).

stronge, adj.: requiring great effort, difficult (3833).

stryffe, adj.: requiring strife, or strong effort (1829).

styff(e), adj: see *stiff(e)*.

stylle, adj., adv.: see *stille*.

stynt(e), stent(e), v.: cut short, cease, stop (3246); abstain from moving, stay (1033, 3947); pause in a journey (986); pret., *stent(e)*.

swayne, n.: a young man attending on a knight (711).

sweven, sweyne, n.: a dream, a vision (3170, 3226).

swithe, swythe, adv.: very much (246); very quickly, very rapidly (531, 674); *as swithe as*: as soon as (79, 394).

swonne, swoune, n.: the act of swooning, syncope, a fainting fit (3728).

swoughe, n.: fainting, a swoon (903, 1634).

sye, syghe, v.: see *sene.*

syker, adj.: secure, safe (2741); firm, dependable (2333, 2340).

syne, adv.: since (3864).

synghand, part.: singing (2371).

sythe, sithe, n.: time, occasion (696, 774, 1561).

sythe, sythen, conj., adv.: see *sithe, sithen.*

tane, p. part.: taken, siezed (1967).

tase, v., 3 s. pres.: takes, brings (956).

te, v.: draw, betake oneself, go, proceed (965, 1015).

telde, n.: a tent or pavilion (2624, 2725).

telle, conj.: to the time that, until (3656).

tene, n.: anger, wrath; ill-will, malice (1449).

tene, v.: be vexed, be angry (281).

tent, v., pret.: attended to, minded, took charge of, looked after (3946).

than(e), adv.: then, at that time (1461, 2876, 2944, 3528).

thar(e), v.: need, be under a necessity (2028, 2338, 2426, 3285).

the, pron.: they (1893).

*thede,*n.: a people, race, or nation (1415); a country (51, 2305, 2361).

thedyr, thedir, adv.: thither, to or towards that place (978, 2703, 2979, 2999, 3002).

theighe, conj.: though; in a modified sense nearly meaning "if" (1985).

thereof, adv.: from or out of that (1038).

thewe, n.: custom, individual habit or manner (1081).

think, v.: seem, appear (635, 768, 3829); pret., *thought.*

tho(o), pron.: those (352, 448, 1151, 1942, 3079).

tho(o), adv.: at that time, then (186, 249, 313, 976, 1020).

thore, adv.: there, at that place (1342, 1736, 2005, 2070, 2388).

thought to, p. part.: intended for (1655).

thouȝth, thowȝ, adv., conj.: though, in spite of the fact that, although (2881, 3257).

thro(o), adj.: stubborn, obstinate, persistent (589, 2184, 2879);
    angry, wroth (1525); keen, eager (2389).

throw, adv.: throughout, through the whole extent (1061).

thrye, adv.: thrice, three times (383).

thryve, p. part.: excellent, worthy, noble (589).

thynne, adj.: sparsely occupied or peopled (2598).

tidandis, tydandis, tydyngis, tithandis, tithingis, tithyngis, tythyngis,
    -es, n., pl.: tidings, reports, news, intelligence, information
    (542, 641, 703, 784, 1966).

tille, tylle, prep.: to (191, 817, 1771, 1780); to or for the purpose
    of, to become, as (637).

to, conj.: to the time that, till, until (374, 3437).

toforne, adv.: before, previously to, earlier than (3608).

toke, v., pret.: delivered, handed over (2713).

tone, art. + num.: the one, as opposed to the other (2797, 3253,
    3384, 3710).

tother, art. + num.: the other (3710).

totorne, p. part.: injured, lacerated, rent (763).

triacle, n.: a medical compound for treating venomous bites
    and other poisons (864).

tronchon, n.: a fragment of a spear, the shaft of a spear; a short
    thick staff, a club (3071).

trone, n.: throne, seat of state (3789, 3944).

trotted, v., pret.: trotted, went or moved quickly (3339).

trouthe, n.: faithfulness, good faith, one's faith as pledged or
    plighted in a solemn agreement (927).

trow, v.: trust, believe (1031, 1154); suppose, imagine (1177);
    feel sure (1171); 2 s. pres., *trowiste*; pret., *trowyd*.

twight, v., pret.: plucked, pulled, drew with a sudden movement
    (1038).

twynne, num.: *in twynne*: in two parts or divisions (2211).

tydandis, tydyngis, tythingis, n., pl.: see *tidandis*.

tyde, n.: time, season, age, occasion (54, 241, 365, 834, 2081).

tyte, adv.: quickly, soon; *as tyte*: as quickly, immediately (3713);
    as tyte as: as soon as, as readily, willingly (488).

undediste, v., 2 s. pret.: reduced to nothing, undid (1152).

undyrtyme, n.: the third hour of the day, about 9 a.m.; tierce (2807).

unfayne, adj.: not glad or delighted, sorry, reluctant (2691).

unhend(e), adj.: discourteous, impolite, ungentle, rude, rough (1001, 1081).

unkouth, adj.: unknown, foreign (851).

unneth(e), adv.: scarcely, hardly, barely (2820, 2857).

unsad, adj.: free from sadness (1508).

unsaught, p. part.: ?not sought or asked for (3189).

unso(u)nde, *unsownde*, adj.: not sound, unhealthy, diseased, suffering from wounds or injuries (2859, 3343, 3387).

untylle, prep.: to, unto (3858).

vayne, n.: *in vayne*: to no effect, uselessly, vainly (1110).

venquesshe, v.: win or gain (a battle or other contest) (1465).

verely, adv.: in truth or verity, truly (1339).

vilanye, n.: conduct befitting a villain, shameful wrongdoing (1163); disgrace, dishonour (1456).

viser(e), n.: visor; the front part of a helmet, covering the face, which could be raised or lowered (1557, 1612).

voute, n.: a vault; an enclosed space covered with an arched roof (972).

wacche, n.: one who watches, a sentinel, the body of soldiers constituting the guard of a place (2605).

waden, v., 3 pl.: walk through water or some other liquid, wade (2235).

waite, *wayte*, v.: watch, have under observation (74, 1779).

wake, v.: remain awake, stay awake to watch or protect, keep watch (2591); keep vigil (in a church, by a corpse), wake (750, 3571).

walowed, v., pret.: roll about, or toss and tumble from side to side, usually while lying down (3931).

wan, v., pret.: won; in religious use: redeemed (2439).

wanne, adj.: of the sea: lacking light, gloomy, dark (3465).

ware, *wore*, *were*, v., pret.: were (30, 483, 769, 1346, 2604); subj., *ware*, *wore*.

warke, n.: work, act, deed, business (3285).

warne, v.: forbid, refuse to allow (3011); exclude, prevent, hinder (3040).

warynge, *werrynge*, ger.: warring, the action of making war (2932, 2975).

wawe, n.: wave, a movement of the sea, the ridges of that movement (3465).

wede, n.: clothing, dress, apparel (2639, 2655); armor, mail (83, 176, 778).

wederes, n., pl.: kinds of weather; weather (2470).

welde, v.: rule or reign over, govern, command (920, 2917, 3263); use, have the use of (101, 1928, 3405).

wele, n.: wellbeing, the opposite of woe, happiness (8, 530, 1823, 2964, 3026, 3788); advantage, profit (2969).

wele, *well(e)*, adv.: well, nearing thoroughness or completeness (103, 412, 2812); fully, completely (690, 1140, 1692, 1841, 2303, 3668); fittingly, properly (1175, 3052, 3104, 3697); fairly, considerably (2111, 2221); with good reason (2140).

wellaway, *wellawo(o)*, *weilaway*, int.: an exclamation of sorrow or lamentation (652, 740, 820, 860, 1410).

welle, adj.: happy, in good estimation (1616, 3203).

welney, adv.: well nigh; very nearly (3062).

welvette, n.: velvet, a silk fabric with a short, dense, smooth piled surface (2615).

wemen, n., pl.: women (2300).

wend(e), *wound(e)*, v.: alter the position or direction of; turn, direct or betake (oneself) (1538); go off or away, depart (2844, 2932); change one's mind; go, proceed, journey, travel (1753); *wend for no walle*: not give away, not succumb in a conflict (2698); pret., *wente*; imper., *wendyth(e)*.

wene, n.: doubt (548, 1680, 1758, 1822, 2546).

wene, v.: think, suppose, surmise, believe, expect (422, 686, 865, 2926, 3054); pret., *wende*, *wente*.

wenge, v.: avenge (2217).

wente, v., pret.: see *wene*, *wend(e)*.

were, v.: wear, be dressed in, have on (2791); dress oneself habitually so (3030).

wer(r)e, n.: war, armed conflict between two forces (1695, 2205, 2247, 2395, 2417).

werrynge, ger.: see *warynge*.

wessche, v., pret.: washed, cleansed with water or other liquid, bathed a wound (2855).

wet(t)e, wote, v.: know, have knowledge of, be aware of (1452, 1537); find out, ascertain, learn, hear (1717, 3567); imper., *wete*: be assured (1857); 2 s. pres., *woste*; pret., *wist(e), wyste.*

wetterlye, wytterly, adv.: clearly, plainly, certainly, undoubtedly, truly (1381, 1452).

wex, v.: grow, increase, advance (2207); become, turn (762, 951, 1870, 3777); pret., *wexe*; p. part., *wexyn.*

whan, adv.: when, at the time at which (1367, 3304).

whedyr, adv.: whither, to what place (3512, 3513, 3603).

where, conj.: whether (as a simple interrogative), if (480, 1987).

wight, wyght, n.: a person, a human being (107); *no wight*: none, not a whit (128).

wight, adj.: strong, courageous, vigorous, active (460).

wight(e)ly, wyghtely, adv.: bravely, stoutly, valiantly (2822); quickly, swiftly (513, 3289).

wis, v., imper.: show, point the way, guide, conduct (3414).

wische, v.: wish, desire (2603).

wiseliche, adv.: with wisdom, sound judgment, sagacity, discretion (1158).

wist(e), wyste, v., pret.: see *wet(t)e.*

wite, wyte, v.: blame, reproach (492, 1153, 2398, 2880); 2 s. pres., *witeste.*

withe, prep.: by (1778).

witte, n.: the mind (787, 914, 1359, 1574).

wo, n., adj.: misfortune, trouble, a grievous or sorrowful state, sorrow (8, 1451, 1891); grieved, miserable, sorrowful (1975, 1985).

wode, adj.: out of one's mind, insane, mad (275, 384, 662, 1172, 1710).

woke, n.: week, seven days (2111).

wold(e), n.: command, control, possession, keeping (745, 3233).

wolle, v.: will (97, 98, 133, 140, 1495).

wondyd, iwoundyd, p. part.: wounded, injured (934, 3434).

wone, n.: abundance, plenty; *in wone*: in abundance, plentifully (1083).

wone, v.: dwell, live, inhabit (137, 332, 2445, 2446, 3636); pret., *wo(u)nyd.*

wonne, n.: place of habitation, dwelling place (3377).

wonnyng, ger.: place of habitation, dwelling place (3561).

woodely, adv.: madly, wildly (3191).

worche, v.: work, do, perform (sth.) (3683).

wore, v.: see *ware*.

worship(pe), *worshyp(pe)*, n.: the condition of deserving or being held in honor or esteem (1152); distinction, renown (35, 2845, 2933).

worshipped, *-id*, p. part.: honored; honored with gifts; treated with respect (1551, 1569).

worshippfully, adv.: with due honor (1117).

worthe, *worthy*, adj.: strong, powerful (2545, 2559).

worthe, v.: become, become of, happen to (1817); get up, on, or upon (a horse) (782).

wote, *woste*, v.: see *wet(t)e*.

woughe, n.: wrong, injury, harm (1333, 1365, 1638).

wound(e), v.: see *wend(e)*.

iwoundyd, p. part.: see *wondyd*.

wount, v., pret.: was wont or accustomed (26).

wo(u)nyd, v., pret.: see *wone*.

wowyd, v., pret.: wooed, courted (1012).

wrake, n.: suffering, as from retribution or punishment (948); hostility, mischief (935); pain, misery (1092, 1181); ruin, destruction (1695, 3567).

wrothe, *wrothely*, adv.: wrathfully, angrily, wrothly, furiously (1349, 1838).

wyght, n.: see *wight*.

wykke, adj.: wicked, severe (3365).

wylanlyche, adv.: villainously, vilely, in the manner of a villain (1156).

wynne, n.: joy, pleasure, delight (3788).

wynne, v.: get, obtain, acquire, gain, procure (1830).

wyste, v., pret.: see *wet(t)e*.

wyte, v.: see *wite*.

wythsayne, v.: contradict, deny (a fact or statement) (2406).

wytterly, adv.: see *wetterlye*.

y-, occasional prefix with p. part, or pret.: see under second letter.

ya, *ȝa*, adv.: yea, indeed; a mere introductory interjection, emphasizing the statement following (79, 1626, 1880).

yare, *ȝare*, adj., adv.: ready, prepared (218, 253, 349, 1121); quickly, promptly, immediately (3536).

yat, n.: a gateway, a gate of a castle (2743).

yche, adj., n.: see *iche*.

ychone, pron. phrase: see *ichone*.

yede, *yo(o)de*, v., pret.: went, went away or out, proceeded, took one's course (81, 346, 667, 986, 1331).

yeff(e), *yeve*, v.: give, confer, deliver, hand over, present, assign, allot (88, 269, 2643, 2728, 2815); pret., *yafe*, *yaff(e)*, *gaffe*; 3 pl. pres., *gyffen*; 2 s. pres., *ȝevyth*; subj., *yeffe*, *yiffe*; imper., *yif*; p. part., *yeve*.

yeld(e), v.: give back, restore, hand over, surrender, submit (924, 1131, 1319, 2139, 3705); pret., *yolde*; p. part., *yolden*.

yen, *yȝen*, *eyne*, n., pl.: the organs of vision, the eyes (1349, 1557, 2083, 2203, 2437).

yif(e), *yiff(e)*, conj.: if, on condition that, unless (199, 1627, 1709, 2077).

yift, n.: gift, a thing given, present (3045).

ylke, adj.: see *ilke*.

ylle, *ille*, n.: evil, harm, injury; misfortune, disaster, distress; as v.: to give oneself ill; to grieve (821, 1324, 1356, 1419); as adv.: ill, evil (3013).

yolde, *yolden*, v., p. part.: see *yeld(e)*.

yone, adj.: yon, that one there (3300, 3424).

yo(o)de, v., pret.: see *yede*.

yt, pron.: see *hit*.

yvell(e), *yevell*, *evyll*, adj.: troublesome, painful, difficult (619); miserable, wretched (477, 1412); as n.: evil, evil thing (3617, 3852).

yvory, n.: ivory (2359).

GLOSSARY OF PROPER NAMES

When a name appears repeatedly throughout the poem, only a few line references are given.

Ag(g)rawayne, Agravayne, Agraveyne: a brother of Gawain and enemy of Lancelot (59, 73, 1676, 1692, 1696).

Arthur: legendary king of Britain (5, 88, 95, 121, 227).

Ascolot, Ascolat: a place in southwestern England between Camelot and Winchester (297, 548, 645, 747, 1136).

Aumysbery: modern Amesbury in Wiltshire, just north of Salisbury (3569, 3954).

Aveloune: a legendary island to which Arthur goes after his final battle (3516).

Banndemagew: a knight and supporter of Lancelot (2564).

Barendowne: a place in Kent between Dover and Canterbury (3094, 3592).

Bedwere: a knight, supporter of Arthur and brother of Sir Lucan (3386, 3400, 3442, 3447, 3486).

Benwicke, Benwyk(e): legendary city and land of which Lancelot is king. It is on the continent, probably in France; France and Gawnes are tributary to it (2305, 2474, 2534, 2707).

Bors, Boert(e) de Gawnes, Gawnys: a brother of Lancelot and king of Gawnes (230, 273, 432, 464, 476).

Bretayne, Bretayen: in this poem, Great Britain (2513, 3376, 3377, 3553).

Canturbery: modern Canterbury in Kent (2982, 3019, 3088, 3119).

Cornwa(y)le: Cornwall in southwestern England (3267, 3275, 3295).

Dover, Dower: modern Dover in Kent (3042, 3055, 3589, 3794).

Ector, Estor: a knight and king, and brother of Lancelot (299, 301, 305, 472, 477).

Evwayn(e): a knight (106, 107, 109, 122, 129).

Fraunce: France, probably just the area around Paris, since it is tributary to Benwick (2486).

Gaheries, Gaheryes, Gaherys: a brother of Gawain (1722, 1931, 1940, 1962).

Gaheriet, Gaheryet: a brother of Gawain (1674, 1722, 1931, 1940, 1962).

Galehod, Galehud, Galyhud: a knight and supporter of Lancelot (43, 225, 261, 2572, 2587).

Gawayn(e), Gaweyne: Arthur's nephew and lieutenant (536, 540, 545, 570, 576).

Gawle: Gaul, the ancient name of France (2487).

Gaynour, Gaynor(e), Genure: Guinevere, Arthur's queen and Lancelot's lover (421, 515, 835, 879, 901).

Glassynbery: modern Glastonbury in Somerset in southwestern England (3960).

Joyus Gard(e), Joyes Garde: a castle belonging to Lancelot in northern England (1669, 2044, 2079, 2108, 2110).

Kamelot: the legendary seat of Arthur's court, apparently in southwestern England (420).

Karl(l)yll(e): modern Carlisle in Cumberland near the Scottish border (2257, 2327, 2349).

Kerlyon(ne): modern Caerleon in Monmouth in southeastern Wales (2466, 2529).

Kent(e): Kent in southeastern England (2982, 3019, 3267, 3275, 3295).

Launcelot(t)e, Launcelett du Lake, de Lake: best of Arthur's knights, Guinevere's lover, and king of Benwick (27, 53, 62, 65, 69).

London: London (2992, 2996, 3800).

Lucan de Bot(t)el(l)er(e): a knight, supporter of Arthur, and brother of Bedwere (2631, 2636, 2695, 2703, 3232).

Lyonell(e), Lionelle: a knight, brother of Lancelot, and king of France (230, 281, 432, 486, 667).

Mador: a knight, probably from Scotland (883, 889, 1449, 1466, 1490).

Mordre(i)d, Mordreit(e): Gawain's half-brother, illegitimate and incestuous son of Arthur; usurper of the throne of England (1675, 1810, 1832, 1862, 1904).

North Gales: North Wales (2580).

Rome: Rome in Italy (2248).

Rowchester: modern Rochester in Kent, southeast of London (2255).

Salysbery, Salusbury: modern Salisbury in Wiltshire in southern England (3148, 3597).

Scottis: Scots, the people of Scotland (2099).

Walys: Wales (2099, 3147).

Wynchester: modern Winchester in Hampshire in southern England (42, 93, 340, 395, 2984).

Yngland(e), Ynglond(e), Engelond: England (347, 2090, 2098, 2249, 2256).

Yreland: Ireland (2098).

SELECTED BIBLIOGRAPHY

Branscheid, Paul, "Über die Quellen des Stabreimenden Morte Arthure", *Anzeiger* to *Anglia*, VIII (1885), 179-236.

Briquet, C. M., *Les Filigranes: dictionnaire historique des marques du papier* (Geneva, 1907).

Bruce, J. Douglas, "The Middle English Metrical Romance 'Le Morte Arthur' (Harleian MS 2252): Its Sources and Its Relation to Sir Thomas Malory's 'Morte Darthur'", *Anglia*, XXIII (1901), 67-100.

Donaldson, E. Talbot, "Malory and the Stanzaic *Le Morte Arthur*", *SP*, XLVII (1950), 460-472.

Ellis, George, *Specimens of Early English Metrical Romances*, ed. by J. O. Halliwell (London: Henry G. Bohn, 1848).

Essays on Malory, ed. by J. A. W. Bennett (Oxford: The Clarendon Press, 1963).

Göller, Karl Heinz, *König Arthur in der Englischen Literatur des späten Mittelalters* (= Palaestra Untersuchungen aus der Deutschen und Englischen Philologie und Literaturgeschichte, CCXXXVIII) (Göttingen: Vandenhoeck und Ruprecht, 1963).

Griffiths, E. T., *Li Chantari di Lancelotto* (Oxford: Oxford University Press, 1924).

Kane, George, *Middle English Literature: A Critical Study of the Romances, the Religious Lyrics, "Piers Plowman"* (London: Methuen and Co., Ltd., 1951).

Malory's Originality, ed. by R. M. Lumiansky (Baltimore: Johns Hopkins Press, 1964).

Matthews, William, *The Ill-framed Knight* (Berkeley, Calif.: Univ. of California Press, 1966).

Maynadier, Howard, *The Arthur of the English Poets* (Boston: Houghton Mifflin Co., 1907).

Moorman, Charles, *The Book of King Arthur* (Lexington: University of Kentucky Press, 1965).

La Mort le Roi Artu, ed. by Jean Frappier, 3rd ed. (Paris: M. J. Minard, 1964).

Le Morte Arthur, ed. by J. Douglas Bruce (Early English Text Society, Extra Series, 88) (London, 1903).

——, ed. by Frederick J. Furnivall (London: Macmillan Co., 1864).

——, ed. by Samuel B. Hemingway (Boston: Houghton Mifflin Co., 1912).

Morte Arthur: Two Early English Romances (New York: E. P. Dutton and Co., 1912).

Mossé, Fernand, *A Handbook of Middle English,* trans. James A. Walker (Baltimore: Johns Hopkins Press, 1952).

Ritson, Joseph, *Ancient Engleish Metrical Romanceës* (London· W. Bulmer and Co., 1802).

Scudder, Vida D., *Le Morte Darthur of Sir Thomas Malory and its Sources* (New York: E. P. Dutton and Co., 1921).

Seyferth, Paul, *Sprache und Metrik des Mittelenglischen Strophischen Gedichtes "Le Morte Arthur" und sein Verhältnis zu "The Lyfe of Ipomydon"* (= Berliner Beitrage zur Germanischen und Romanischen Philologie, VIII) Berlin: C. Vogts Verlag, 1895).

Vinaver, Eugene, *Malory* (Oxford: The Clarendon Press, 1929).

——, ed., *The Works of Sir Thomas Malory* (Oxford: The Clarendon Press, 1947).

Wanley, Humphrey, *Catalogue of the Harleian Manuscripts* (London: 1808).

Weston, Jessie L., *The Chief Middle English Poets* (Cambridge, Mass.: Riverside Press, 1914).

Wilson, Robert H. "Malory, the Stanzaic *Morte Arthur,* and the *Mort Artu*", *MP,* XXXVII (1939), 125-138.